Empty Pastures

Empty Pastures

CONFINED ANIMALS AND
THE TRANSFORMATION OF
THE RURAL LANDSCAPE

Terence J. Centner

University of Illinois Press
Urbana and Chicago

The drawings in chapters 2–12 were prepared by Laura Alfonso
and are used with her permission.

Library of Congress Cataloging-in-Publication Data
Centner, Terence J.
Empty pastures : confined animals and the transformation of the
rural landscape / Terence J. Centner.
p.   cm.
Includes bibliographical references (p.   ) and index.
ISBN 0-252-02895-3 (cloth : alk. paper)
1. Agriculture—United States.
2. Agricultural ecology—United States.
3. Agriculture—Environmental aspects—United States.
4. Landscape changes—United States.
I. Title.
S441.C45   2004
636'.00973—dc21   2003012760

To Mary Ann, Ann Marie, and John.
and to Mom, Dad, Harry, and Jean

Contents

Illustrations follow page 102

Abbreviations

AFO	Animal feeding operation
BMP	Best management practice
CAFO	Concentrated animal feeding operation
CNMP	Comprehensive nutrient management plan
CRP	Conservation Reserve Program
EPA	Environmental Protection Agency
NPDES	National Pollutant Discharge Elimination System
TMDL	Total maximum daily load
USDA	United States Department of Agriculture

Empty Pastures

The Centner Farm

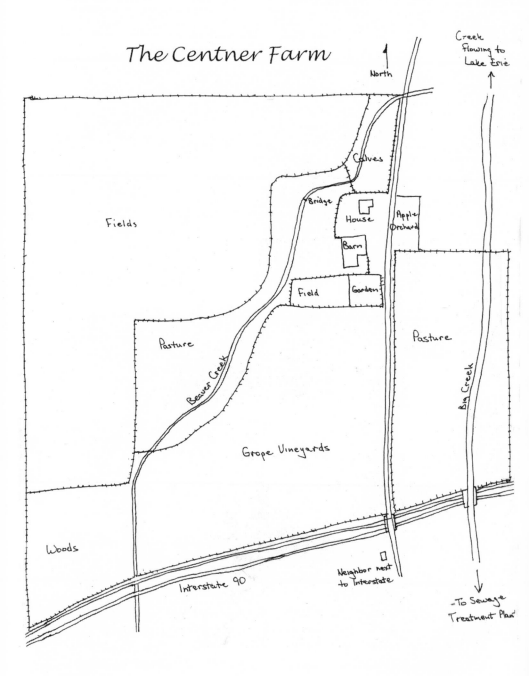

1   Serenity in the Countryside

It's my final journey home. Deep guilt envelopes my chest as I recognize that I could have prevented this passing. How did the circumstances unfold so quickly? My parents and siblings gave me the chance to prevent this separation. My wife supported the use of our funds to buy myself peace. Yet I had failed to comprehend what was happening, to recognize the end was near, and then I decided that the price to change the result was too high. Thus, this last pilgrimage.

I drive along the interstate trying to concentrate on the traffic rather than imagine what might have been. My mind drifts to the beautiful views of rolling farmlands and wooded hillsides. I find solace in the landscape I love—rural America. Yet the bucolic countryside is bittersweet. It reminds me of what is being lost and what I have given up. Perhaps I need to let my wife drive, so that my daydreaming does not interfere with the family's safety. For my head is bursting with memories, with contrition for not having preserved the legacy of my family's farm.

I can picture my great-grandfather, who immigrated to this country in the 1860s. He arrived not speaking a word of English, and the expenses of bringing a family of four from a rural village in northern Germany to America surely depleted his resources. How he must have struggled to earn the funds required to establish the family's bulwark—a farm—in this country. And then my grandfather. As a first-generation American, he was marked with a drive to succeed. And he did. The little sugar maple trees he planted in the yard provided shade for the farmhouse over an entire century. Seventy years after drainage tiles were laid in the back fields, they still carry away water to allow spring cultivation.

With Dad's marriage, my grandfather decided seventy years on the farm were enough. He willingly stepped aside to allow a new generation to take control, unfettered by paternal pressure. This is this farm that I remember, that prompted an eternally

*enduring love of the countryside. The land and buildings pro-
vided my family a refuge for over 130 years; now I'm making my
final journey there. Final because the family farm has been sold.
This trip is my last chance to amble through the empty pastures,
over the fields, and through the woods. Thereafter, the family's
inheritance will end.*

Family farmers are part of our country's heritage.[1] They helped found our
country, and their labor and independence have championed the values
of democracy. I grew up on a farm, where my childhood revolved around
farm chores and youth projects involving food production. The chores
required lots of hard work, but being a part of such an occupation and
lifestyle offered real satisfaction. As others have stated, farmers tend to be
friendly, healthy, honest, and hardworking.[2] Farming is the most basic of
occupations: humble, necessary, and worthy of support. Agriculture is like
"motherhood and apple pie"—it is America.

A New Agenda for Agriculture

But rural America is not simply about farming. It provides not only abun-
dant food but also clean water and air resources and recreational opportunities for people living in more populated areas. Many Americans take
pleasure in viewing or visiting the countryside for relaxation and relief
from the hassles of their lives. Given the attributes of our rural areas, the
public has an interest in agriculture and what occurs in our countryside.

In some cases, this interest is expressed through legislation on farm
policy, such as the 2002 farm bill that provides economic support to agricultural producers. Increasingly, however, the public has focused on environmental and social issues involving industrial agricultural production.
Modern animal- and crop-production practices involving bioengineered
genes, weedsprays, insecticides, antibiotics, and liquid-waste lagoons are
seen as creating unacceptable problems. Agricultural pollutants, animal-
production practices, and genetically modified crops threaten the quality
of our water and other natural resources and the diversity of living organisms, yet producers tend to resist efforts to address these issues because the
solutions would cost them too much.

One of the major problems involves aggregations of thousands of
animals at individual production facilities and congregations of such facilities in particular regions. In place of diversified crop and animal pro-

duction, with green pastures for livestock, we have large numbers of animals in enclosed areas. Some of these confined animals live in less than acceptable conditions. Moreover, aggregations of animals pose problems for the sustainable use of their manure as a production input, since excessive amounts of nutrients from animal manure are already impairing the quality of our water resources.

This book addresses changes in agricultural production that have contributed to today's public issues. By reviewing what has occurred, we can discern how we might attempt to return to the greener pastures some of us viewed as youths. While we cannot really turn back the clock—and I don't want to—we can do more to help persons living in small towns and rural areas cope with their economic difficulties. By analyzing regulations governing the production of crops and farm animals, we can suggest revised regulatory policies to secure cleaner water and more acceptable animal-confinement practices. We can provide greater assistance to farmers who conserve resources, own areas that cleanse water and air, and accord us the countryside we so admire.

My Recollections of Rural America

My recollection of the family farm starts with Dad's stories about the farm of his youth. In the 1920s cows, horses, pigs, chickens, ducks, and geese roamed the barnyard. The farm's first motorized vehicle appeared after Dad was born. My own memories of the same settings date back to the 1950s and 1960s. Progress meant the farm was specializing in milk and Concord grapes, and except for the cows, all the farm animals were gone. Today the farm has changed even more. Flowers bloom in the barnyard. Wild animals have free range over the fields and woods. The farm is a picturesque landscape with its sole income coming from grape production. By focusing on two areas of my family's farm, I can describe some of the changes that have contributed to current concerns.

Eastern Creek Lands

Years ago the eastern part of the farm consisted of a low-lying creek bottom rising up to the road. Dad knew the area as a densely wooded area around Canadaway Creek. The creek meandered through the floodplain between huge black willow trees. Yet at times it was foreboding. During the nineteenth century the creek's waters had threatened to undermine the farmhouse, so my great-grandparents moved the house two hundred yards westward across the dirt road to escape the surging waters. Pieces of old bricks from the former house's foundation appear each time the field is plowed.

The eastern creek lands I knew in the 1950s were a pasture consisting of a flat area where the creek changed channels and higher elevations on both sides. The pasture contained a few old willow trees, black walnuts, and two sugar maples. With the greening of the pasture each spring, Dad would fix the fences destroyed by the creek's ice floes and floodwaters. Soon hungry cows devoured every edible green leaf and blade they could reach.

From our front yard we could see the entire pasture, beyond which stood a handsome red barn (owned by one of my great uncles), distant trees, and the foothills of the Alleghenies. We could also spot distinct farmsteads among the partially wooded hillsides. During the summer we could watch storms drop their rain on the hillsides to the south. In the spring and fall we could see the white snow on the higher elevations when our ground was bare. What a glorious view of pastoral landscapes.

By denuding the vegetation, the cows helped the creek erode new channels through the flat bottomland. The snowmelt from the upland hills combined with rains from the paved areas of the upstream village to produce mighty spring floods. The high waters of the unruly creek would carry gravel and large trees from upstream locations and deposit them in our pasture. A new channel would be formed as an earlier one became clogged with dead trees or too much gravel. Leftover pools might contain polliwogs, and the floodplain contained an engrossing array of rocks, shale, and other debris. During some summers earthmoving equipment would be brought in to remove loads of gravel that were sold for construction projects.

Today only part of the pasture remains. Yearly mowing lets the upland portions retain their grasses and forbs. Without cows or other human intervention, Mother Nature has returned the creek bottom to a floodplain setting. Woods dense with poplar, willow, locust, black walnut, and other tree species block the vista of my uncle's barn and the distant hills.

The Westerly Fields

The farm's westerly fields, sometimes including vineyards, lie beyond a pasture cut by the meandering Beaver Creek. This creek is smaller than Canadaway, but it was big enough to make it difficult to reach the farm's western half. A few old trees along its banks offered the cows shade during the summer. Of course, up to the late 1940s the pasture fed grazing horses, too. Mostly cows used the creek, however, and as they stopped for a drink, they often relieved themselves, polluting its waters.

This creek changed as well. When Dad was a boy, reaching the westerly fields meant fording the stream. Horses would strain to pull their loads of hay, grain, and Concord grapes down through the creek and then up the rutted pathway to the barn. Finally, in the 1940s, a concrete bridge was constructed over the creek. Regularly maintained, it has endured to tie the farm together.

Among the most noticeable features of the westerly fields were the leftover oxbow banks of Beaver Creek's former channels. For years the stream's abrupt embankments were too steep to be incorporated into a field, so they remained havens for native plants and wildlife. Blossoming wildflowers, blackberries, sumac, and saplings thrived on these banks. Weedsprays, such as Roundup, had not yet been deployed to eradicate bothersome weeds. In the 1960s Dad decided to get rid of these obstacles. He had a bulldozer brought in to grade the natural areas into slopes gentle enough to work. Today the westerly fields are a contiguous expanse that is mowed yearly to prevent the fields from returning to woodlands.

Beyond the westerly fields were neighboring fields and then the railroad. Our view of the rural landscape stretched for a half-mile westward. In the 1960s we used to count the railroad cars per train. We watched in awe the trainloads of automobiles traveling from Detroit to the New York and New England markets. Now the open vistas and distant views are gone. As with the eastern creek lands, the older views here have disappeared. The western fields are now surrounded by newly wooded areas of our western neighbor, which block the former views and limit the vistas to the farm itself.

Today's Countrysides

A drive, bike ride, or walk through today's countryside will not bestow the sights my dad and I remember from our youths. The barnyards, pastures, fields, and animals of yesteryear no longer make up part of our countryside. The small farms have been consolidated into larger holdings. Farmsteads have expanded or been demolished, and fences have been removed to aggregate fields. Pastures have been recruited for crop production or allowed to return to woodlands. Swamps and marshy areas have been drained and fields have been leveled to create more acreage for planting. Our agricultural countryside has become a food machine.

American farmers prospered during World War II, and the countryside of the 1950s reflected their good fortune. Towns were bustling as agricultural enterprises flourished from wartime sales. Unknown to rural Americans, however, a new agricultural era was dawning. Progress was bringing specialization and new hazards for the countryside. Over the next fifty years, family farms with multiple types of crops and farm animals would disappear. Pastoral landscapes would give way to intense cultivation in some areas and abandoned fields and buildings in others. Low commodity prices resulting from increased productivity would drive farm families from the countryside. This is the legacy of our competitive marketplace and governmental farm programs.

The more pronounced change, however, has been the exit of farm families from rural areas. Except for those in areas that have been developed for business and residential purposes and locales suitable for second homes, rural communities have been forsaken. Rural residents have moved to suburban and urban areas for educational and social opportunities. As transportation systems and options for securing inputs and selling products have multiplied, marketing and supply businesses have consolidated and moved farther from farms. A few large machinery dealers have replaced dozens of hometown dealers. A couple of marketing operations exist where a score of similar firms existed in the early 1960s. Processing facilities are gigantic, so not many are needed. Our farm population has decreased, so fewer than 5 million Americans reside on farms,[3] and less than 11 percent of the rural population is classified as rural farm.[4]

In some locations hobby farms and other noncommercial agricultural operations continue the farming practices that were familiar to previous generations. But these are not real farms and cannot be said to represent American agriculture. Today's agricultural countryside is an endless expanse of row crops inundating commodities markets with foodstuffs, immense animal factories producing animal products, and concentrated fruit and vegetable production areas dependent on pesticides to control fungal and insect pests.

In fact, we produce so much food that we agonize over how to curb production. Politicians—invoking conservation—develop programs to pay farmers not to plant certain crops. Under the recent Conservation Reserve Program, our country idled 36 million acres from production to reduce surplus foodstuffs and control soil erosion and safeguard water quality. To offset low commodity prices, the 2002 farm bill provides $180 billion to agriculture.[5] Many of these funds are paid as crop subsidies that encourage overproduction and lead to low crop prices. We help multinational corporations export our food and develop programs to give away foodstuffs to qualifying foreign countries. Ironically, even as we provide financial assistance to our agricultural economy, our farmers and politicians rail against foreign governments that subsidize their own agricultural producers, claiming unfair competition and discrimination.

In developing the most productive agricultural system in the world, we have eliminated the bucolic countryside of yesteryear. Our acclaimed food machine has replaced variety with monotony. Intensive cropping systems have decimated insect and bird populations. We have allowed commercial agricultural production to release significant amounts of pesticides, animal wastes, and excess nutrients into our nation's waters. In the name of efficiency, we compromise the health of agricultural workers through exceptions to health regulations and through production practices involving high concentrations of pesticides and unhealthy air.

The Confinement of Animals

Animal agriculture has experienced monumental consolidation during the past forty years. Today many farm animals are concentrated at a few individual farms and in locations with convenient transport to processing facilities. Whatever its benefits, this trend also introduces problems. The aggregation of animals at animal feeding operations (AFOs) and in particular regions has exacerbated their potential for environmental degradation. Animals generate manure, which needs to be recycled as an input in the production process. Although historically manure has been used as fertilizer, this may not be possible when too many animals are raised in a single facility or locale. The acreage may be too small to recycle the manure. In addition, animal-waste lagoons accompanying animal production beget terrible smells that offend nearby property owners.

Many farmers are aware of their operations' by-products and have adopted measures to eliminate egregious problems. But the public's aspirations for cleaner water and air suggest that more stringent environmental regulations will be advocated. Farming will become more expensive. Some farmers will alter their activities or adopt appropriate technology to comply with the enhanced environmental requirements, a few will forgo expensive changes and break the law, and others will simply quit farming.

Faced with all this, many have sought to address concerns about environmental degradation and animal health associated with large-scale animal production. A major impetus to do more about AFO pollution came in September 1999 when Hurricane Floyd caused massive flooding in North Carolina.[6] Reports indicated that the floods damaged 430 AFOs,[7] with between twenty and thirty animal-waste lagoons discharging their contents into adjacent waters. This environmental disaster led governments to assess their regulations and take additional steps to control pollution from animal waste. Others are concerned about the confinement of animals in overly small cages or spaces and the lack of individualized attention they may receive at large production facilities.

Specialization and Monocultures

Although much farm acreage has been deserted, some areas—especially the Midwest—display prolific stands of soybeans and endless fields of corn and other grains. Where fields slope, carefully planned terraces curving along natural physical contours add to the grandeur of the countryside. Other areas display huge well-kept structures for livestock. These environs attest a bounteous agricultural landscape.

Such productive systems, although beautiful, nevertheless mask the destruction of natural resources. Because of specialization and commercialization, many of today's agricultural areas present a monotonous landscape lacking the variety of plants and animals our parents and grandparents knew. Three generations ago native plants, several crop species, and various livestock populated almost every farm. Even during the 1950s multiple crops and farm animals were readily apparent in these rural areas. Today's landscapes are less beautiful and less interesting—and perhaps less healthy. Depending on the locale, a weekend drive into the countryside may disclose fertile fields of crops and large buildings confining animals, but we are unlikely to see native weed species, green pastures, a variety of crops, or any domestic farm animals.

We might, however, find more wild animals of a few species. It is common to see deer at daybreak or dusk as we drive in rural areas. Indeed, protection from hunters and the deer's ability to adapt to new landscapes have allowed their populations to soar to the highest numbers of the past one hundred years. Raccoons, Canada geese, ducks, wild turkeys, and black bears have markedly increased in number as well.[8] But these animals tend to inhabit areas abandoned by agriculture; few animals live where row-crop production predominates.

Also missing from the landscape are some previously common plant species. Running buffalo clover, northern wild monkshood, small whorled pogonia, American hart's-tongue, and Meads's milkweed have declined so precipitously that experts feel their survival may be threatened.[9]

Detecting Other Changes

Our other senses can show us changes beyond those apparent to vision. What about the smells and the sounds of the countryside? How have they changed? Pretend it's summer. What changes do our noses discern? First, the sweet-smelling flowers prevalent during my youth are gone—gone from fencerows, ditches, pastures, and meadows. We are losing species diversity. Modern agriculture has removed these menaces in favor of vast expanses of cultivated crops. Second, the aromas of sweet drying grass are absent—farms no longer need hay. Specialized production has removed cows and other hay-consuming animals from rural America. Concomitantly, the stinky smells of animal manure are missing from most areas— there are no animals on most farms. But before we celebrate this last change, consider its consequences. In the few locations animals are present, their large numbers can make their stench overwhelming, and disposing of their wastes presents a real challenge. Many large confinement facilities have too many nutrients and emit foul odors that neighboring property owners find objectionable.

Next, let's listen to the noises around us. What sounds can we hear in rural America? Are there many insects? Of course not: most have been poisoned so that they cannot harm our crops. Can we hear many birds? Not if we're in an area of intensive row-crop production. Most avian species cannot survive in monocultures, which lack required food and habitat. Other bird species have been relegated to nonagricultural areas, since today's farming is not conducive to their reproduction. Grassland and shrub-land nesting birds especially have suffered significant declines.[10] The loss of fields and excessive browsing by deer has removed so much vegetation that some bird species lack suitable nesting sites. We may have trouble viewing species such as the mountain plover, eastern meadowlark, western meadowlark, northern bobwhite, Henslow's sparrow, grasshopper sparrow, sage sparrow, Franklin's gull, and dickcissel due to precipitous declines in their numbers.[11]

Can we hear any farm animals, tractors, or other machinery? In most places few sounds come from the countryside. We will hear tractors and other mechanized farm equipment during short periods of planting, spraying, and harvesting. Discerning the "moo," "oink," or "cackle" of domesticated farm animals will be more difficult: most rural landscapes lack them. Pastures, barnyards, and pigsties are no longer needed. Cows, horses, pigs, and poultry are seldom seen or heard. The pastures associated with conventional farming are uncommon in today's agricultural countryside. As pastures have vanished, so too have the native mammal, insect, and bird species and domestic animals that used to populate these landscapes. Instead, we have created "ecological sacrifice zones," where we allow intensive agricultural production and sacrifice native species.[12]

A Changing View of Agriculture

A special relationship between agriculture and democracy has influenced legislative bodies in their deliberations on issues relating to agriculture. Because food is required for human life, farmers are hard-working individuals, our healthy agriculture contributes to a strong economy, and agricultural foodstuffs help our balance of trade, legislatures view agricultural legislation as quite important. Congress has long supported commodity producers with legislation to help maintain stable prices and provide adequate food reserves. State legislatures are receptive to bills that agricultural groups champion as needed to preserve rural America. Examples include "right-to-farm" laws[13] and statutes establishing liability for accidents with horses.[14]

While most still view agriculture favorably, changes in production practices have altered rural landscapes and led to changing attitudes. Environmental problems caused by pesticides and bursting hog-waste lagoons have led to a new perception of production agriculture. The pollution of rivers and groundwater has alerted the public that agriculture is not simply a conservator of picturesque landscapes. Concerns about contamination from animal agriculture, loss of biodiversity, overuse of antibiotics in producing farm animals, and health problems accompanying odors from manure are leading to increased regulation.

As a result, agriculture is losing its privileged status. Specialization and the industrialization of animal production have eroded the generalities that have long been associated with agriculture. Citizens are wondering whether their ideas of farmers constitute a pastoral myth now being dissipated by technological advances. Can the positive perceptions of agriculture continue to influence the decisions of legislators and regulators? And who will benefit from those decisions? Although many farm families deserve special dispensation, families supporting themselves entirely by farming constitute an endangered species. Since three-quarters of our farms are noncommercial units with operators whose occupation is not primarily farming, many people have difficulties identifying real farmers.

Moreover, the small percentage of Americans who live on farms has altered the political landscape, so that farm interests are not as weighty as they used to be. The special status that agriculture enjoyed throughout the first two hundred years of our history is disintegrating. Perhaps that's as it should be. Agricultural production as it exists today may no longer be entitled to exemptions or regulatory concessions. The lax oversight of agricultural pollution may not be justified given the more stringent environmental provisions prescribed for other businesses and industries.

Special Dispensation with Respect to the Environment

Given that American farmers are the most efficient and productive farmers in the world, should they retain a privileged position with respect to environmental legislation? Surely our farmers can be good stewards of our nation's resources while producing sufficient food. People expect their food to be plentiful and varied. Many Americans thus feel that agriculture can afford to do more to safeguard the environment and provide humane facilities for animals. The fact that environmental stewardship practices will lead to slightly higher food prices does not justify allowing existing contamination to continue.

Nevertheless, a considerable number of agricultural interest groups remain fixated with preserving productivity to the detriment of environmental quality and social issues. A part of the agricultural sector I will call the "farm lobby" advances several arguments for treating agriculture differently. The farm lobby claims that unless farmers can engage in activities and practices that some may find offensive, they cannot compete in the world marketplace. It further claims that higher food prices would harm the poor. Others maintain that farmers should not be expected to implement conservation measures because more than half our farms are unprofitable—thousands of farmers have been driven off their farms in the past decade. Overall, however, these positions are losing credibility as conditions change.

This does not mean that the public lacks support for our nation's agricultural sector. The 2002 farm bill shows that legislators will support this needy sector of our economy during hard times. But many Americans realize that more stringent environmental controls will not reduce our ability to enjoy a wide variety of safe and healthy food products. Recognizing that production agriculture does not operate in a vacuum, the public is demanding greater social accountability. Agriculture has a broader responsibility to our nation than just producing food; specifically, it should preserve natural resources for future generations. Unwelcome noises, smells, and pollutants from agricultural activities are viewed as the misuse of natural resources rather than the unfortunate but necessary by-products of agricultural production. Offensive activities that adversely affect others' property, bodies of water, and recreational activities can be proscribed. With respect to certain afflictions, regulators are taking action.

NOTES

1. Ronald D. Knutson, J. B. Penn, and William T. Boehm, *Agricultural and Food Policy,* 3d ed. (Englewood Cliffs, N.J.: Prentice-Hall, 1995), 10.

2. Ibid.

3. U.S. Department of Agriculture, *Agricultural Statistics 1977* (Washington, D.C.: USDA, 1977), 434; U.S. Department of Agriculture, *Agricultural Statistics 1998* (Washington, D.C.: USDA, 1998), IX-12; U.S. Department of Agriculture, *Support Services Bureau: Executive Summary* (available at <http://www.info.usda.gov/cfr/ex_sum.htm>).

4. U.S. Department of Commerce, *1990 Census of Population: Social and Economic Characteristics* (Washington, D.C.: U.S. Department of Commerce, 1990), table 1.

5. Carolyn Lochhead, "Fate of Huge Farm Bill Crucial to California," *San Francisco Chronicle,* Dec. 6, 2001, p. A1.

6. "Floyd's Legacy: Record Losses in North Carolina" (available at <http://www.CNN.com>), Sept. 22, 1999.

7. Ibid.

8. James Conaway, "Eastern Wildlife: Bittersweet Success," *National Geographic,* Feb. 1992, pp. 66–69; Michael Kenna, "White-tailed Deer," *National Geographic,* Feb. 1992, pp. 70–81.

9. David W. Lowe, John R. Matthews, and Charles J. Moseley, *Official World Wildlife Fund Guide to Endangered Species of North America* (Washington, D.C.: Beacham, 1990).

10. Robert A. Askins, "Population Trends in Grassland, Shrubland, and Forest Birds in Eastern North America," *Current Ornithology* 11 (1993): 1–34; Curtis H. Flather, Stephen J. Brady, and Michael S. Knowles, *Wildlife Resource Trends in the United States,* Forest Service General Technical Report RMRS-GTR-33 (Washington, D.C.: USDA, 1999).

11. Fritz L. Knopf, "Declining Grassland Birds," *A Report to the Nation on the Distribution, Abundance, and Health of U.S. Plants, Animals, and Ecosystems* (Washington, D.C.: U.S. Department of the Interior, 1995); Askins, "Population Trends," 1–34.

12. Laura L. Jackson, "The Farm, the Nature Preserve, and the Conservation Biologist," in *The Farm as a Natural Habitat: Reconnecting Food Systems with Ecosystems,* ed. Dana L. Jackson and Laura L. Jackson (Washington, D.C.: Island, 2002), 40.

13. Neil D. Hamilton, *A Producer's Legal Guide to Nuisance, Land Use Control, and Environmental Law* (Des Moines, Iowa: Drake University Law Center, 1992).

14. Terence J. Centner, "The New Equine Liability Statutes," *Tennessee Law Review* 62 (1995): 997–1039.

2   Changes in Agricultural Production

*S*omething *always requires attention on a dairy farm. Some chores, no matter how detestable, just have to be done. For me one of these was cleaning manure from the barn. Each morning during winter—when the cows had to remain in the barn—my brother and I had to help clean out the manure before we went to school. Our alarm would waken us before dawn. We would dress in our barn clothes and boots and walk to the barn. While my brother backed the tractor and manure spreader out of the barn, I would get bales of hay out of the hay mow.*

My dad, brother, and I would then work together to get the manure in the spreader. The manure lay in the gutter behind the cows and needed to be loaded into the manure spreader. To do so, we used a conveyer belt in the bottom of the gutter where the cows deposited their waste. At the flip of a switch an electric motor would pull the belt toward the manure spreader, and the manure would drop off the belt into the spreader. The setup was simple, but it suffered from a major defect. Because the barn sat on flat ground, the belt and manure had to go up an inclined chute. The incline was just steep enough that the manure would occasionally slide off the belt and remain in the gutter or the chute.

With one day's accumulation of manure in the spreader, my brother would drive it to a field. Once he engaged a gear, the manure would be flung out over a six- to eight-foot-wide area behind the moving tractor and spreader. My brother needed to pay close attention to any wind during this operation. As long as he drove into the wind, the manure would hurtle into the air away from the tractor and driver. When the wind was at my brother's back, however, the manure would pelt him and the tractor, causing a most unpleasant mess, including a manure-encrusted jacket badly in need of washing.

After we completed this chore, we would return to the house for a shower and dress for school. Mom would have our breakfast waiting and watch the clock. Soon we were off to the schoolbus stop a quarter of a mile down the road. Amazingly, despite snowstorms and other adverse weather, we always managed to stay on schedule, catch the bus, and have a normal day at school.

The manure-handling practice of my childhood exemplifies a formerly normal farming practice now recognized as contrary to good stewardship. Spreading manure daily throughout the winter risks contaminating water. Animal farms need manure-holding facilities so that applications of manure occur during appropriate times of the growing season.

Other practices and procedures, both voluntary and those required by governmental regulations, have similarly altered agriculture. Many of the changes result from the industrialization of agriculture. Our food-production system has been transformed from a labor-intensive to a mechanized one. Technology, specialization, and innovation have wrought an industrialized agricultural-production system that can grow more food on less land. We need fewer farmers—less than 2 percent of our population (the lowest percentage in the world)—to produce all the food we need as well as large amounts for export.[1] But this industrialization has created adversities and new challenges. Thousands of producers have had to exit farming. Agricultural-commodity producers have sought billions of dollars from Congress to idle farm acreages, support rural lending institutions, and apply conservation practices. Legislative bodies have needed to enact legislation to protect people and property from poisons and pollutants associated with new production practices.

Production Wonder

To appreciate what has happened to the rural landscape, we need to highlight some aspects of agricultural production associated with its changes. Our founding fathers were attuned to agricultural production, and to this day agriculture continues to enjoy a favored status. The current assistance for farmers may be traced to a visionary senator from Vermont who in 1865 introduced a bill to establish the Land Grant University System to assist Americans in rural areas. That same year Congress created the U.S. Department of Agriculture (USDA). This was followed in 1887 by legislation providing funds to support agricultural-experiment stations. With these measures in place, the federal government assumed an important role in rural development. Funding of local cooperative extension staff followed in 1914.

Federal legislation was instrumental in enabling American agriculture to become the efficient and productive industry we all know. The support system of land grant universities, the Cooperative Extension Service, and other legislatively mandated measures continue to contribute to the transformation of our agricultural sector. Innovative programs encourage individual farmers to adopt new production practices, implement conservation measures, and consider better ways to market their products. Indeed, many foreign countries, in an attempt to duplicate the perceived prosperity of our farm sector, have copied American farm programs, support mechanisms, and food-protection policies to bolster their agricultural production.

The celebrated status of American agriculture casts farmers as leaders in the adoption of new technology. No other country has done so much to make agricultural production less labor intensive. American agricultural firms have been pioneers in developing and marketing new food products, as well as processing and packaging them. We have also taken great strides to ensure that our food will be safe for consumption; in fact, American innovations in food safety have helped people everywhere to avoid food-borne pathogens and diseases. At the same time, scientists have helped firms learn how to eliminate or utilize waste by-products. Millions of tons of plant and animal by-products are being used as ingredients for alternative goods or as inputs in production processes. America is a production wonder, incorporating science, technology, and efficiencies to market cheap foodstuffs all over the world.

Lobby Powerhouse

Our production wonder is not simply the result of market forces. Farmers have come together in various organizations to pool resources and gain power. This began in 1868 when the farm community established the first working Grange in Fredonia, New York. For nearly one hundred years Granges were significant social and educational appendages of many farm communities. More significantly, Granges provided a stage for the development of other agricultural support groups, such as agricultural marketing cooperatives and local Farm Bureau units. Foundations provided by the Grange allowed farm organizations to evolve into forceful groups that actively espoused agricultural agendas.

The New Deal programs of the 1930s showed farmers that governments can provide safety nets and other benefits through friendly legislation. Although farmers may advocate less legislation, they have not hesitated to request governmental assistance when facing crop failures, bad prices, natural disasters, or other maladies. When farmers were suffering under the bankruptcy options in the 1980s, the farm lobby managed to secure a new bankruptcy option.[2] *Fortune Magazine,* in its "Power 25" survey, has noted that the American Farm Bureau Federation is one of the nation's most powerful lobbing groups. In 2001 the Farm Bureau was rated to be a more powerful lobbying group than the American Bankers Association and the National Governors' Association.[3]

Every federal farm bill enacted demonstrates the farm lobby's ability to advance legislation. The debate surrounding the 2002 farm bill showed how compelling the farm lobby could be in garnering support for agriculture. But does this lobby represent all farmers or just some agricultural interests?

A recent study using 1999 data found that a majority of federal farm payments go to the producers of eight major crops: wheat, corn, barley, oats, sorghum, rice, cotton, and oilseeds (soybeans).[4] Since feed grains are among these commodities, the subsidies indirectly benefit livestock producers, who pay less for feed inputs. Supports for fruits and vegetables, food items important to our health, are notably missing.

Moreover, the figures show that much of the federal farm money is not going to assist family farm operations. Fifty-two percent of these federal funds were paid to the largest 8 percent of our farms.[5] Small farms, which constitute fully 76 percent of our nation's farms, received only 14 percent of our farm payments.[6] Because it is linked to production, this support program is regressive, benefiting large-scale farmers more than small farmers.[7] This situation has prompted the comment that farm subsidies "are paying for the demise of family farms."[8] By receiving over half our federal farm subsidies, farmers with large operations have had funds to buy out their smaller neighbors.

Another major controversy concerns the geographic distribution of agricultural-support funds. One-half of federal farm payments goes to farmers in six states: Iowa, Illinois, Texas, Kansas, Nebraska, and Minnesota.[9] Some of the other important agricultural states receive little funding.

Farm groups may be even more successful at the state level. In the 1960s and 1970s they successfully advocated antinuisance legislation to protect farms from nuisance lawsuits. Confronting a legal decision from Nebraska regarding livestock warranties, the farm lobby persuaded the Nebraska Legislature to revise its provisions on implied warranties of animal health. Within a decade nearly one-half the states adopted similar amendments.[10] Within six years following the addition of a new equine liability law by the Washington State Legislature in 1989, over thirty states enacted equivalent statutes to help shield horse owners from liability for equine accidents.[11] Farm groups are very adept at championing agricultural issues, especially those for large producers and agribusiness firms.

Poverty Despite Agriculture's Productivity

Agricultural programs and innovations have not produced universal prosperity. Indeed, these programs and accomplishments have spelled difficulty for many farmers. As a result, in many rural areas a traveler will see abandoned buildings and farm equipment. In other areas deserted farms and overgrown fields abound. First, governmental programs for agriculture have fostered consolidation of farms and the resultant depopulation of rural America.[12] Other financial issues have played a role here, too. As recently as the 1980s, 10 percent of farm borrowers had difficulty making their loan payments,[13] and more agricultural banks failed in 1987 than in any year since the Great Depression.[14] Beyond that, adjusting to technological and other changes in our market economy has presented smaller farmers considerable challenges. Facing individual adversity, a considerable number of commercial farmers abandoned farming for other occupations—or perhaps gave up on life altogether: statistics showing higher suicide rates in rural areas than urban areas suggest just how stressful the lives of rural residents can be.[15]

In addition, agriculture has experienced adjustments familiar to manufacturing and retail businesses as well. Farm operations have been streamlined to accommodate a world marketplace. Economies of scale have dictated changes that include consolidation: grow or become uncompetitive. Thus, while our nation's agricultural accomplishments bespeak success, the benefits to rural areas have been bittersweet. Not only do some rural areas suffer from high unemployment, but low agricultural commodity prices and unprofitable farms have contributed to the demise of many rural communities.

Why are farmers leaving agriculture? The main reason is money. Existing facilities cannot generate enough income to support a family. Farm families often try to adapt by having a spouse take an off-farm job. Statistics show that the operator, operator's spouse, or both are working off the farm at 55 percent of our farms.[16] Sometimes, however, the family cannot cover expenses and keep the farm afloat even with this extra income. Thousands of farmers have had to sell their family farms to pay their bills. Others have forgone health care and nearly starved—even though they are commercial food producers. It's a painful paradox: our bountiful agricultural production is accompanied by a good number of farmers who cannot earn enough to feed their own families.

Forgoing the Farm's Resources

As a result of these financial difficulties, many farmers cannot properly care for their farm's resources. Without sufficient funds, a farmer may not take suitable measures to maintain natural resources and prevent environmental degradation. To compete in the international marketplace, producers have expanded their operations, creating monocultures of row crops and grains and huge concentrated AFOs (CAFOs). While these operations have economic advantages for individual producers, the gains do not extend to the rural communities, since monocultures and CAFOs tend to degrade the environment and reduce the quality of life.

To meet financial obligations, producers are forced simultaneously to expand and to cut corners on environmental stewardship practices. The failure to adopt soil retention measures has resulted in unacceptable soil erosion. Pesticides carelessly applied have ended up in water supplies. Because of the excessive quantities of manure they produce, CAFOs entail major problems with odors and pollution.[17] In addition, phosphorus and nitrogen from AFOs are impairing water quality, and the widespread use of antibiotics in animal production is accelerating the development of resistant bacteria.

This environmental degradation accompanies increased energy consumption. CAFOs require transporting large quantities of grain for feed. Specialized crop production consumes large amounts of energy in the form of petroleum and fertilizer inputs. Fertilizers, chemicals, fuel, lubricants, and electricity are estimated to constitute 24 percent of cotton's total production costs[18] and 44 percent of production costs for corn grown in the Midwest.[19] It is estimated that agriculture uses about 6 percent of all energy consumed in the United States.[20]

These economic and social conditions suggest that farming is not the blissful occupation many assume it to be. Agricultural production requires long hours and uninteresting routines. Overproduction and keen competition place severe financial stress on operators. Banks and big businesses directly or indirectly dominate farming operations and their production decisions. Farmers no longer expect to pass their homesteads to heirs. Rather, some farm families hope that their sons or daughters will find more desirable careers off the farm.

Looking at Our Farms

Turning to the farms themselves, what changes do we see in rural America? Many of us like to think of our countryside as containing individual family farms, with farmsteads being a prominent part of this scene. We have visions of farmsteads consisting of identifiable barns, agricultural outbuildings, and a farmhouse. A few stately trees would grace many of these buildings. Today such rural landscapes are rare. We have a greatly reduced number of identifiable agricultural operations. Statistics show that the number of farms has dwindled by 50 percent since 1960.[21] Today we have only about 2 million farms.[22]

This figure, however, is misleadingly high. Our government defines a farm as any place that produces and sells (or ordinarily would sell) $1,000 or more of agricultural products during a year. Under this definition, a person who grows and sells more than $1,000 worth of vegetables is a farmer, even though the person may work full time elsewhere. A lawyer or physician who raises horses for leisure and in a typical year markets a few animals valued at more than $1,000 is a farmer.

Under this definition of a farm, three-fourths of our farms are small or part-time operations with less than $50,000 in sales.[23] Farms with less than $50,000 in sales are called "noncommercial" farms. While these units might be called farms, they generally serve as hobbies, tax writeoffs, or real estate investments by individuals who enjoy the countryside. These farms are also seen as significant in preserving countryside from urban sprawl, but in many cases they simply defer it. When buyers appear, hobby farms are often transformed into subdivisions.

Given their numbers and locations near urban and suburban areas, hobby farms are the most recognized type of farm in America. Many people enjoy the amenities these farms afford. As our government defines things, however, our typical family farmer has an unprofitable operation, doesn't produce much, and has a nonfarm job.

To evaluate changes in agricultural production more accurately, we might consider only farms generating more than $50,000 in products, known as commercial farms. For these farms, agricultural production is generally the operator's principal means of livelihood. Approximately one-fourth of the farms in our country fall in this category—500,000 farms. Commercial farmers are responsible for 91 percent of our agricultural production.[24] Thus, seen from a production standpoint, commercial producers are most representative of American agriculture.

Governmental statistics group our largest farms in the category of "superfarms," which possess an astonishing productive capacity. According to some estimates, only about 3 percent of our country's farms account for more than one-half our agricultural production.[25] The largest 1 percent of our farms produces 30 percent of our food. As their production outputs suggest, these industrial-type facilities operate on a scale that dwarfs most of our family farms.

These statistics illustrate the difficulty of defining operations that should be considered farms. This difficulty in turn complicates determining who qualifies for farm-assistance programs. So what is the future of the American family farm and rural America? American families will continue with their hobbies or investments on farms, but agriculture has moved to a new stage of economic development. Instead of having a viable rural America, we simply have a few farms in the countryside.[26] The farm images depicted in history books, by our grandparents, and through my youthful observations are nearly impossible to find. Most of our agricultural products are produced by hybrid farm factories.

Perhaps the exodus of farm families from rural America differs little from the flight from core urban areas. But what will happen to our depressed rural communities? Many view those who seek recreational pursuits and retirement communities as potential saviors. An influx of new folk, with a disposable income to buy their desired styles of life, often provides the main source of funds for revitalizing rural areas. But these rural communities will differ from those known by our grandparents. They will be founded not on an agricultural economy but rather on a service economy.

Land Use in the Countryside

These descriptions of farm units allow us to consider changes in land use. The concentration and specialization of agricultural production means that rural American landscapes are less diverse today than at any other time since our nation's founding. Cropping monocultures have replaced the former checkerboard formed by fields of assorted crops. Large-scale agricultural production has made it more economical to raise only one or two crops—the same crops raised by neighboring farmers.

Animal production has changed the landscape as well. Few animals other than cattle are produced outdoors, but even ranging cattle are brought to confined feedlots for fattening. Dairy cows are relegated almost entirely to confined free-stall situations. Poultry and hogs are generally confined in cages, pens, and buildings. In an even more momentous change, commercial producers have moved to areas and states where low costs let them compete in a difficult marketplace: poultry to the Southeast, cattle to the Great Plains, and dairy cows to California. Economies of scale have led to the concentration of animal production in some areas and the demise of production in others.

Farm Acreage and Size

While total U.S. cropland acreage has remained relatively constant,[27] the acreage actually used for farming has shrunk. Cropland, pasture, and land for other farm uses have dropped 15 percent since 1960, so that less than 1 billion acres is devoted to agricultural production.[28] About 50 percent of all land in the United States is managed by farmers and ranchers,[29] but today's farmers are using less land for production than at any time since 1925.[30] In the East much of the acreage removed from farming has returned to forests or been appropriated for recreational activities and suburban development.

The average farm comprises 435 acres,[31] but this figure masks the changes that have occurred. After all, the average includes 1.5 million hobby farms. Today's commercial farms average 1,082 acres.[32]

CAFOs in our most important livestock states have greatly affected land use as well. First, we can identify the states with the most animals: cattle (Texas, Nebraska, Kansas, Oklahoma, California, and Missouri); hogs (Iowa, North Carolina, Minnesota, Illinois, Indiana, and Nebraska); dairy cows (California, Wisconsin, New York, Pennsylvania, Minnesota, and Texas); and chickens (Georgia, Arkansas, Alabama, Mississippi, North Carolina, and Texas).[33] Next, let's consider the acreage used for agriculture in these states today and forty years ago. Six of these states—Alabama, Georgia, Mississippi, New York, North Carolina, and Pennsylvania—have lost more than 35 percent of their farm acreage. Another four states—Arkansas, California, Indiana, and Wisconsin—have reported reductions greater than 10 percent.

It is thus not surprising that our rural countryside looks very different in several of these leading livestock-producing states. A lot of acreage has been removed from agricultural production, often being converted to commercial, industrial, and residential uses. In some locales, however, much of it has reverted to forests or other vegetation beneficial to the environment.

Numbers of Animals

Are farmers raising more animals? Have domestic consumption and exports of meat products led to larger herds and flocks over the past forty years? The results may be surprising, for only poultry has experienced much growth.

The data for cattle reveal little change in the numbers of animals. Cattle numbers (excluding dairy) have increased by about 10 percent. But this is only part of the story. Kansas, Oklahoma, and Texas (three of the six states with the most cattle) have experienced a more than 50 percent increase in cattle numbers.[34] That is, a tremendous concentration of animals in traditional cattle-producing states has accompanied diminished numbers in other states.

Hog numbers show different yet similar trends. On the one hand, data disclose that hogs have decreased nearly 11 percent overall. Illinois, Indiana, and Missouri (three traditional hog-producing states) have experienced major declines in the numbers of animals.[35] On the other hand, North Carolina has experienced a 484 percent increase in the number of hogs.

More startling, the number of dairy cows has diminished by 45 percent over the past forty years. Except for California, the leading dairy states have each lost more than 25 percent of their dairy animals. Minnesota has 55 percent fewer dairy cows. California, however, has experienced a 91 percent increase in dairy cows. That is, most states have far fewer dairy cows, but California has a lot more.

If we look in the countryside for farm animals, changes are very conspicuous. Farms involved in the production of animals have virtually vanished, especially in states that are not major producers of animals. Since 1960 hog farms have decreased by 92 percent; farms with dairy cows, by 93 percent; poultry operations, by 71 percent; and cattle operations, by 55 percent. This explains why we see few animals in the countryside. Moreover, the concentration of animals at individual locations helps explain why animal wastes have become a major issue.

Technological Change and Profits

Technological change has affected agriculture much as it has other businesses. If new technology succeeds in reducing production costs, those who adopt it early on benefit from a competitive advantage. As business operators, commercial farmers tend to be well aware that new ideas and technology can help them increase their revenues. American farmers have been innovators and pacesetters in adopting technology, including biotechnology. Those who fail to adopt new superior production technology generally have difficulty remaining profitable. (Hobby farms and specialty crops, such as organic products, may provide exceptions to this rule.) At the same time, given the inherent risks of agricultural production, farmers are wary of new ideas, which may be impractical. Many farmers have discovered that not all innovations can be effectively incorporated into commercial production.

Although farmers initially benefit from adopting new cost-saving technology, lower commodity prices eventually eliminate these profits. Those who fail to adopt measures to lower production costs, including consolidation, find themselves even more uncompetitive. In addition, many forms of technology require investments in machinery or equipment that can be recouped only if the equipment is used in large-scale production. If a farm's limited production output will not cover the cost of investing in the new technology, the farmer is forced to cease production.

Adopting technology or new practices to meet environmental objectives also places operators at a disadvantage. Farmers often incur costs without receiving higher prices for their goods, forgoing financial gain to provide environmental protection even though they do not recoup the loss. For example, if farmers decide to keep their livestock out of streams, they must pay for fencing. They will also lose forage. The problem is that, although farmers bear the costs of these protective measures, others reap the benefits.

In fact, economic pressures may lead farmers to ignore environmental costs that their activities impose on others. Their profit-maximizing objectives often lead individual farmers to leave environmental issues at the watershed, regional, national, and global levels outside their decision-making processes. Farmers don't set harming the environment as a goal, but their profit-maximizing behavior often damages neighbors and regional resources.

Because what maximizes individual's profits doesn't always serve society's interests, governments must occasionally intervene. Our legislative bodies have enacted an array of laws to reduce or ban the discharge of pollutants onto land or into air and water. Other regulations forbid activities that are likely to inflict damage on others. Governments also mandate stewardship practices safeguarding natural resources. Until we require farmers to internalize environmental costs, they may be expected to engage in activities that degrade our environment.

Specialization

Agricultural producers have specialized for the same reasons that industrial and commercial sectors have done so: efficiencies and profits. The advantages in efficiency are straightforward: any one person or farm will typically lack the time, resources, and knowledge to pursue multiple agricultural activities, unless they are complementary, whereas specialization lets individuals use precise information and resources to achieve a single goal. Advances in science, geographical information systems, and technological projections have helped foster this trend toward the specialized production of animals and crops.

Economics

Economic forces drive specialization. Under capitalism, we seek the full use of production inputs; in addition, economies of scale favor specialized production facilities. Farmers and ranchers have thus aggregated farm animals into large CAFOs to reduce the range of necessary equipment, facilities, operators, and expertise. Specialization in one or two crops has similar advantages. Many farmers have lowered their production costs in this manner, forcing smaller, less efficient production units out of business.

Farmers used to raise multiple crops and feed some of their grains to their own livestock, a way of farming that involved growing different sets of crops. These farmers would use some fields for relatively soil-conserving crops, such as wheat, oats, and barley, and other fields for more intensive row crops, such as cotton, soybeans, and corn. To optimize plant growth, they would deposit their farm animals' manure on fields that were deficient in nutrients. Such production practices tended to conserve soil resources.

Specialization has changed all that, with each region playing to its strength. Farms with productive soils raise mostly row crops, and areas with a competitive advantage for livestock concentrate on animal production. Specialization has also reduced crop rotation of grass, alfalfa, and other soil-conserving species. Today's producers thus forgo some conservation practices practiced two generations ago.

Traditional agriculture, with multiple crops and animal species, helped manage risk: if financial returns from one crop were down, those from other crops might carry the farmer through to the next year. Contemporary commercial farmers often lack this security. They have no backup source of income. Many of today's farmers specialize in one or two agricultural pursuits, tying their income to a single commodity group. More than two-thirds of American farms depend on a single commodity or commodity group for 50 percent or more of their total sales.[36] Of the specialized farms, 50 percent focus on beef cattle, and 20 percent produce a cash grain crop.

Running against the old adage, these farmers have put most of their eggs in one basket. Low prices for a commodity, adverse weather leading to the destruction of the particular crop, or an agronomic miscalculation affecting the entire crop can eliminate the majority of a farmer's income during a bad year. Specialization has resulted in "feast or famine" conditions. When prices for the commodity are up, the farmer does fine. When prices are down, hard times can force the liquidation of the farming unit. So specialization offers increased efficiency, but at a cost: if something goes wrong and the crop fails, the farmer can lose everything.

Technology

Advances in technology and biotechnology continue to increase farm productivity. In fact, the past few decades have brought impressive productivity gains. According to one calculation, farmers' productivity increased 36 percent between 1982 and 1994.[37] Although weather and other factors prevent yearly productivity advances, research indicates that agricultural productivity has increased an average of 2 percent per year since 1948.[38] Productivity increases, however, do not guarantee future profits. They offer only the potential to achieve or increase profits in the short term. In the long term, the market adjusts, and competition drives prices down.

Overproduction accompanied by a continued downward trend of agricultural commodity prices has characterized production agriculture. The various production efficiencies that emerged over the past forty years have enabled farmers to reduce costs while growing more food. Because of the superb organization and production of our agricultural sector, we are accustomed to spending an unusually low percentage of our disposable income on food and other agricultural products. Americans spend less than 11 percent of their disposable income on food,[39] a figure lower than that for any other country.

Biotechnology has exacerbated specialization. Recall that, to be adopted, any new technology must offer a productive advantage. Biotechnology offers just such an advantage in the form of more profitable plant or animal species. Such advantageous technologies then generally become widespread. For example, new crop varieties can end up replacing most competing varieties. This in turn introduces risk, for the resulting monoculture increases the crop's susceptibility to a new disease or a climatic adversity.

Specialization of agricultural production has created environmental problems, too. Concentrating animals or crops in an area increases the potential for excessive quantities of substances, discharges, or releases to pollute the surrounding air, water, and land. Where there are large numbers of animals, it is more likely that surplus waste nutrients will damage streams and other bodies of water. In some areas, CAFOs need three times as much land as is currently being used to provide for the efficient use of the nitrogen contained in their manure.[40] Monocultures of corn and other crops present an increased need for pesticides to control insects, weeds, and other pathogens. Meeting this need heightens the chances that pesticides will pollute nearby waters. Moreover, successive production of row crops may exacerbate soil erosion or lead to the depletion of soil resources.

Measuring Our Harvests

With our bounteous harvests, Americans should be happy with our agricultural production. But what price do we pay for this abundance? While we have some of the lowest food prices in the world, we wreak havoc with producers' lives and our environment. And many Americans are asking whether governmental policies might not be partly responsible for some of the deleterious conditions that accompany agricultural production.

Agriculture is so competitive that large factorylike farms are driving typical family farms out of business. What kind of occupation do we have when only one out of four operators is profitable? Why are poverty, stress, and suicide so prevalent in rural America? On the other hand, why do we offer price guarantees to some producers facing low returns due to crop surpluses?

Turning to environmental issues, should we be doing more to diminish pollution from erosion and animal wastes? We have invested billions of dollars in conservation programs, yet agricultural contamination is rampant. We have mandated controls under the Clean Water Act, yet many of our waters are still impaired. Have our programs failed, or do we need to adopt more realistic expectations? Critics argue that agricultural producers are not paying for the pollutants they discharge into streams and the atmosphere. At the same time, we are not paying farmers for the public goods we all enjoy, including aesthetic landscapes, species habitats, carbon capture, and community jobs.

More important, many people wonder what current agricultural production means for our future. Are farmers degrading the environment rather than engaging in sustainable practices? Research suggests that soil erosion damages our natural resources, engineered genes threaten genetic diversity, and CAFOs endanger human health. Over the next few years Americans will no doubt become more concerned about the problems that accompany factory-farm production. We may attempt to temper unacceptable risks and environmental damages that large farms are foisting on our society and resources.

NOTES

1. Emery N. Castle, *Agricultural Industrialization in the American Countryside* (Greenbelt, Md.: Henry A. Wallace Institute, 1998).

2. Susan A. Schneider, "Recent Developments in Chapter 12 Bankruptcy," *Indiana Law Review* 24 (1991): 1357–78.

3. "The Power 25 Top Lobbying Groups," *Fortune,* May 28, 2001.

4. General Accounting Office, *Farm Programs: Information on Recipients of Federal Payments* (Washington, D.C.: GAO, June 2001).

5. Ibid., 29.

6. Ibid., 12.

7. Organisation for Economic Co-operation and Development, *Agricultural Policies in OECD Countries: A Positive Reform Agenda,* COM/AGR/TD/WP(2002)19/Final (Paris: OECD, Nov. 2002), 32.

8. Bill Hambrecht, "Congressional Coalition Fights to Change Farm Subsidies: Eastern Senators Want More for Conservation," *St. Louis Post-Dispatch,* Nov. 25, 2001, p. A1.

9. Ibid., 5.

10. Donald L. Uchtmann, M. E. Sarhan, and H. Charalambous, "Do Statutory Exclusions of Implied Warranties in Livestock Sales Immunize Sellers from Liability?" *Oklahoma City Law Review* 8 (1983): 221–45.

11. Terence J. Centner, "The New Equine Liability Statutes," *Tennessee Law Review* 62 (1995): 997–1039.

12. Jake Thompson, "More Aid for Small, Medium Farms Favored in Poll," *Omaha World-Herald,* Nov. 14, 2001, p. 16a.

13. Kathryn Marie Dudley, *Debt and Dispossession* (Chicago: University of Chicago Press, 2000), 8.

14. Ibid., 8.

15. Angie Wagner, "Downside to Rural Life—High Suicide Rates," *Atlanta Journal-Constitution,* Oct. 15, 2000, p. A-18.

16. Robert A. Hoppe et al., *Structural and Financial Characteristics of U.S. Farms: 2001 Family Farm Report* (Washington, D.C.: USDA, May 2001), 33.

17. Ted Williams, "Assembly Line Swine," *Audubon Magazine,* Mar.–Apr. 1998, pp. 26–33.

18. Nora L. Brooks, *Characteristics and Production Costs of U.S. Cotton Farms,* Statistical Bulletin no. 974-2 (Washington, D.C.: USDA, 2001).

19. Linda F. Foreman, *Characteristics and Production Costs of U.S. Corn Farms,* Statistical Bulletin no. 974-1 (Washington, D.C.: USDA, 2001).

20. David Pimentel et al., "Environmental and Economic Costs of Soil Erosion and Conservation Benefits," *Science* 267 (1995): 1117–21.

21. U.S. Department of Agriculture, *Agricultural Statistics 1977* (Washington, D.C.: USDA, 1977), 422.

22. U.S. Department of Agriculture, *Agricultural Statistics 1999* (Washington, D.C.: USDA, 1999), IX-2.

23. Judith E. Sommer, Robert A. Hoppe, Robert C. Green, and Penelope J. Korb, *Structural and Financial Characteristics of U.S. Farms, 1995: 20th Annual Family Farm Report to the Congress* (Washington, D.C.: USDA, 1998), 8.

24. Ibid.

25. Ibid.

26. Steven C. Blank, "The End of the American Farm," *The Futurist,* Apr. 1999, pp. 22–27.

27. USDA, *Agricultural Statistics 1999,* IX-9.

28. U.S. Department of Agriculture, *Agricultural Statistics 1972* (Washington, D.C.: USDA, 1972), 504; idem, *Agricultural Statistics 1999,* IX-2.

29. George M. Boody, "Agriculture as a Public Good," in *The Farm as a Natural Habitat: Reconnecting Food Systems with Ecosystems,* ed. Dana L. Jackson and Laura L. Jackson (Washington, D.C.: Island, 2002), 262.

30. U.S. Department of Agriculture, *Agricultural Statistics 1984* (Washington, D.C.: USDA, 1984), 377.

31. USDA, *Agricultural Statistics 1999,* IX-2.

32. Sommer et al., *Structural and Financial Characteristics,* 8.

33. U.S. Department of Agriculture, *Agricultural Statistics 1998* (Washington, D.C.: USDA, 1998); idem, *Agricultural Statistics 1999.*

34. U.S. Department of Commerce, *1960 Census of Agriculture* (Washington,

D.C.: U.S. Department of Commerce, 1960); USDA, *Agricultural Statistics 1998;* idem, *Agricultural Statistics 1999.*

35. Department of Commerce, *1960 Census of Agriculture;* USDA, *Agricultural Statistics 1998;* idem, *Agricultural Statistics 1999.*

36. Sommer et al., *Structural and Financial Characteristics,* iv.

37. USDA, *Agricultural Statistics 1998,* IX-24.

38. V. Eldon Ball, Jean-Christophe Bureau, and Richard Nehring, "Agricultural Productivity Revisited," *American Journal of Agricultural Economics* 79 (1997): 1045–63.

39. U.S. Department of Agriculture, *Agricultural Fact Book 1998* (Washington, D.C.: USDA, 1998), 14.

40. Laura L. Jackson, "Restoring Prairie Processes to Farmlands," in *The Farm as a Natural Habitat,* ed. Jackson and Jackson, 145.

3 The Production of Animals

My ninth year included the summer of Olie and Ora, when they were both still calves. I was in the barn one evening talking with my dad while he milked the cows. He asked me how the two calves were doing. I checked them out where he had placed them, in a little pasture behind the north side of the house, and reported back. Dad then suggested that I take a scoopful of grain to each calf. Dad wanted to aid their development with some enriched grain feed. The next night he made the same suggestion, and soon it was my summer responsibility. I took two pails of grain to the pasture, crawled through the fence, and walked to the calves. How they loved the grain! The remainder of their diet was grass.

After a few days of walking to Olie and Ora, I found I needed only bang the pails together and they would come to me. A week or two later I found an even easier way to attract their attention. I just yelled "here Olie and Ora." Hearing this simple refrain, they would run to me and the pails. Although I performed this task at roughly the same time each day, Olie and Ora were usually down in the pasture eating grass. But my yell always brought them running. They never failed to come when I called—they were as responsive as the family dog.

> *In fact, they would come whenever I called them, even if I had no grain. They never showed disappointment at not getting grain. The most inflated feeling of control came when I called them and they were eating grass on the other side of Beaver Creek. The banks of the creek were about eight feet high. Olie and Ora had to find a good place to descend, enter the creek, wade through the rocks or navigate the slippery slate, and then bound up on the near side to reach me.*

When I grew up, dairy farmers had a name for every cow. Although the animals had ear tags for identification, herds were small enough that farmers knew the habits and dispositions of each animal. They could identify an animal that needed special care or medical attention. But small herds of dairy cows no longer exist. The farms where they lived have been replaced by farm factories producing milk. In fact, there are fewer dairy farms in our entire country than there are households in St. Paul, Minnesota.

The consolidation rampant within the production of animals has made it difficult to find a yeoman-family farmer. Sure, we have family farms, but given the changes in the industry, they are quite different from the farms I knew through my 4-H dairy project.

Matters of Scale

Much of the animal production in the United States occurs at AFOs, with the largest being designated as concentrated AFOs—CAFOs. Each year fewer than 30,000 poultry farms produce 84 billion eggs, 8 billion broilers, 434 million chickens (other than broilers), and 272 million turkeys.[1] Our 60 million hogs are being raised on 85,000 hog farms. Statistics show that, in Arkansas, an average hog farm has more than 2,700 hogs and an average poultry farm has 274,839 birds.[2] Concentrations in one area, such as hogs in eastern North Carolina, can result in a great deal of waste being applied to acreages in a single watershed.

To produce beef cattle, we use feedlots. Large numbers of animals are brought to these confined areas for fattening. In Texas, our largest cattle-producing state, fewer than 5 percent of the beef operations produce nearly 50 percent of the state's marketed beef cattle.[3] Nearly 80 percent of the largest Texas feedlots are located in the Panhandle.[4] Animals remain in feedlots for five or six months, with each animal producing just under one ton of dry manure solids. In some cases the manure and urine from these feedlots overwhelm the surrounding cropland.

In the pursuit of profits, CAFOs sometimes ignore legally prescribed environmental standards. According to a 1997 environmental study, 88 percent of North Carolina's hog facilities had violated water-quality laws or regulations at least once.[5] In 1998 reporters charged that a majority of California's dairies were illegally polluting water.[6] No wonder the public is concerned: the scale of these operations can create problems with the disposal of their waste by-products.

Visiting a Factorylike Farrowing Facility

I recently visited a modern farrowing facility with 2,400 sows, an operation quite different from those I had seen and heard about as a child. First, entry is restricted to workers and invited guests. To prevent the introduction of diseases, each person entering the confinement buildings must shower and change into clean clothes provided by the business. This procedure applies to every employee, veterinarian, inspector, and guest. When dressed, you leave the dressing room and walk to a room containing pairs of boots. You pick a pair that fits and wear them while in the facility. When you leave, you spray off the boots and leave them in the boot room. The facility uses these security precautions to avoid maladies and diseases that would adversely affect the production of piglets.

Buildings and Animals

The facility consisted of two production barns, one for holding sows before and after they deliver and a second for the actual farrowing. A separate building houses the office, break room, laundry room, and changing facilities. The sows spend most of their lives in the first building, since they are in the farrowing facility for only a little more than two weeks each time they deliver a new litter. The barns have combinations of slatted and wire floors so that all waste falls into holding pits below. These pits are periodically flushed into a lagoon.

The farrowing building includes a hallway, eight farrowing rooms, and areas for equipment, medicine, and utilities. A farrowing room contains forty-eight individual pens, one per sow. Each week about one hundred pregnant sows walk from the first building to the farrowing facility a few days before they are scheduled to give birth. They are herded in groups of five so that employees can prevent any potentially harmful scuffling. In the farrowing room horizontal iron bars confine each sow to the middle of her pen. She can stand up or lay down in this confined area, but her movement is limited to several inches sideways or forward and back. Each week at least two of the farrowing rooms are emptied and power washed. Pressurized water is sprayed on the floor and other surfaces to clean the rooms. The water blows all wastes and other debris into the holding pits below. The rooms are then ready for the next group of pregnant sows. The facility produces about 54,000 piglets a year.

After giving birth to her piglets, a sow lies on her side to let them nurse. Since she is in the middle of the pen, there are areas on both sides exclusively for the piglets. The piglets can run under the bar to reach the sow' udder. After they have fed, they return to their area to relax and sleep. This design minimizes the chance that a sow will accidentally smother a piglet by lying on it.

The farrowing rooms are maintained with utmost care to provide an optimum environment for the sows and piglets. Each sow has her own feed trough and water supply. She is fed twice a day, and the amount of feed is noted (any leftover grain is dumped so it does not get sour). This arrangement allows each sow to eat as much as she wants yet simultaneously avoids waste.

Again, wire floors allow the urine and feces to drop into a holding tank. The pigs thus stay clean and dry. Fans constantly change the air in the room. The odor, although present, remains tolerable because of the continuous supply of fresh air. A climate-control system maintains a comfortable temperature. Since sows like it a bit cooler than the new piglets do, heat lamps provide additional heat on one side of each sow, where the piglets can congregate to be warmer.

A few days after birth, the piglets' ears are tagged and their tails are docked; the males are castrated. Sharp teeth are trimmed so that they do not hurt the mother's teats. The piglets are weaned about fifteen days after they are born. This involves examining each piglet by hand and separating males from females. The piglets are then loaded onto a truck and transported to a feeder facility in another state. With their piglets gone, the sows walk back to the first building. These walks to and from the farrowing building are the only times the sows get any exercise or see sunlight. To eliminate fighting and avoid injuries, sows are confined to individual pens, where they are bred through artificial insemination. Therefore, the sows spend their entire lives confined in pens in these two buildings.

Records

As might be expected, these facilities keep records of all the significant activities occurring there. Every pig is identified by an ear tag. Above each pen holding a gilt or sow a form documents the pig's production information. The date of breeding is noted, and well as the follow-up ultrasound test to certify pregnancy. In the farrowing pens, the date of delivery and number of live offspring are noted. The office also maintains copies of all this paperwork. Key information is transmitted weekly to the marketing firm.

Sows tend to have smaller litters after six or seven deliveries. When their reproductive capacities diminish to a certain point, the sows are culled and sent to the slaughterhouse. New gilts are brought in regularly to replace the culled sows. Detailed records allow the manager to cull just enough sows to keep the facility operating at capacity, letting the owners receive maximum returns on their capital investment.

All this mechanization and recordkeeping creates a facility as automated as is any industrial factory. Breeding sows exist for their reproductive capacities. Their lives are regimented toward the production of offspring to maximize profits, with carefully prescribed controls to keep animals healthy and pregnant. Except for the fifteen days around farrowing, the sows have no social interactions with animals. They never have a choice of food. And these automated production facilities mirror those for other forms of livestock. Facilities for growing hogs and broilers, fattening cattle, and producing eggs and milk also operate under factorylike conditions.

Ownership and Management

The facility I visited is a family-owned, integrated operation situated on over three hundred acres in a rural area. It operates smoothly and has an excellent record of healthy sows and the delivery of healthy piglets. No residential areas are nearby, although one employee lives about one-quarter mile away. The owner resides with his family on a farm about ten miles distant, and the hog farm's manager lives in neighboring community more than twenty miles away.

The owner is not wealthy; in fact, he works hard to keep his business solvent. He is attentive to his family and his kids' activities. When I asked to visit his facility, he readily agreed yet admitted that some of the practices were not animal-friendly. He is not satisfied with the severe restrictions placed on the sows but must employ the practices to be economical.

The owner has entered a detailed marketing contract with a huge agricultural firm. The owner provides the housing and labor and buys all the grain, gilts, and semen from this single agribusiness firm. He also sells the piglets and culled sows to this firm. The manager sends detailed records to the firm each week and must use a veterinarian it designates.

Thus, the entire operation depends on the contract with the agribusiness firm. The firm dictates how the facility is operated and the animals are raised. If the owner fails to follow the stipulated requirements, he will not be offered a subsequent contract. Since there is scant possibility of selling to another firm, the owner's production buildings would be worthless without the contract.

With an operation of this scale, good management is essential. The manager supervises additional employees (both male and female) who tend the sows and piglets; the seven full-time helpers are well versed in all facets of the production operation. All employees are covered by workers compensation. To stimulate performance, the agribusiness firm pays a quarterly bonus to the facility if it meets production goals; each employee then receives part of this bonus. Most of the current employees worked for the owner prior to the construction of the facility, with the manager and another employee having worked in the business for fifteen years.

The strict rules for showering in and out prevent the employees from leaving the facility for meals. Rather, they bring their lunches and eat in a break room in the office building. Surprisingly, this area is not smelly, although it is a bit dreary. The workers have major responsibilities and are dedicated to their jobs. While the chores are the same every day, they must be on the alert for sick sows or piglets and for faulty or broken equipment. The workers must also cover for employees who are ill or on vacation. Holidays are particularly demanding, since the facility continues to operate. The sows give birth to 1,000 piglets every week, and employees have to be there to perform the necessary chores.

The facility is so new that its waste lagoon has never been filled to capacity. An operational spray irrigation system is being used to dispose of liquid waste. At some point solids from the lagoon will need to be removed and distributed on nearby land. Thus, the facility has never been out of compliance with environmental regulations, and its remote location has prevented any problems with its odors. Many CAFOs do not have such a record. Older facilities with lagoons and CAFOs near residential land may have so much manure that they have difficulties conforming to today's environmental standards.

Vertical Integration—Poultry and Pork

Vertical integration, the business arrangement described for the farrowing facility I visited, has constituted a major change in the production of farm animals. This development emerged in the broiler industry in the

1930s. Large feed companies established production contracts with broiler growers. Production contracts are agreements between contractors (integrators or processors) and producers (farmers) involving the joint provision of inputs to the production process. Contractors provide the baby animals, feed, and veterinary services, while producers supply all other essentials for the production of the animals. These contracts evolved to ensure a market outlet for feed supplies, to reduce growers' risks, and to create incentives to produce efficiently. Coordinating various stages of production through production contracts lowers costs.

During the last decade integration has become common in the pork industry. Whereas integration in the poultry industry mainly employs production contracts, the pork industry uses marketing contracts, which are agreements involving the future purchase and delivery of animals under which the producer retains ownership of the animals until delivery. Typical provisions delineate quantities, quality criteria, and delivery schedules. In return, the producer receives an ensured market, a market-based price, and premiums for quality. Marketing contracts allow packers to reduce costs associated with variable supply flows and poor-quality hogs.

Both production and marketing contracts are detailed and leave little to chance. (For example, the facility I visited had to sell its animals to the processor at the price per pound specified in the contract.) Integrators use such contracts to bind growers to established costs and prices. Since any profits above production costs accrue to growers, they have an incentive to produce animals quickly and economically. In turn, integrators can control their costs by determining input and sales prices. Ultimately integrators profit both from supplying inputs to growers and from selling animal products to retailers or distributors.

The normal supply and demand conditions vanish in an integrated marketing system; the touted market economy of capitalism no longer applies. For example, growers often have little choice but to accept the feed prices integrators set via production contracts. For their part, integrators assume that market prices will be high enough to cover their costs. They can alter the terms of future production contracts if feed prices go up, but they may suffer some short-term losses in supplying feed at the terms set by existing contracts. When feed prices go down, integrators generally enjoy short-term profits.

Regarding meat products, integrators bear fluctuations in the market prices. When meat prices go up, integrators reap benefits. When prices go down, they suffer losses. To avoid volatile meat prices and maintain stable restaurant prices for their products, some processors are entering long-term contracts with distributors. This means that integrators have predetermined prices for the inputs they supply to producers, the animals they buy, and the meat products they sell.

AFO Waste

When I was a child, most animals were raised on farms with sufficient acreage for the disposal of their manure as a crop input. While some practices (such as winter manure application) may not have been environmentally correct, animal waste was nearly always used as a fertilizer for crops grown on the farm. On average, animal waste can supply 15 percent of the nitrogen and 42 percent of the phosphorus crops need, with the value of these nutrients approaching $3.4 billion annually.[7]

Today, large CAFOs may generate too many waste products for use on surrounding lands. Farm animals in our country produce thirteen times as much fecal waste (on a dry-weight basis) as humans do.[8] Livestock excretes 5.8 million tons of nitrogen and 1.7 million tons of phosphorus each year.[9] Producers are well aware of the public's concerns and spend large sums to dispose of waste, but problems remain with applying waste at the right time and ensuring that some fields do not receive excessive amounts of waste. Substantial evidence shows excess nitrogen and phosphorus from manure (and cheap fertilizer) causing water pollution and eutrophication (an excess of nutrients) leading to algal blooms and damage to stocks of fish and shellfish.[10] By considering the facilities, equipment, and disposal practices, we can more clearly understand how the production of animals is affecting our landscapes.

Facilities and Equipment

Large-scale animal-production facilities rely on efficient if not automated design. Facilities such as the farrowing operation I visited have controlled ventilation systems and floor surfaces that are either partly or entirely slotted. Although the facility I observed used a flushing system to remove the manure collected under the slotted floors, others employ scraping or pumping to remove the manure. The frequency of the manure removal from the pit depends on the disposal system. Alternatively, some hog-growing units have adopted concrete-slab facilities housing hundreds (or even thousands) of animals. Concrete-slab facilities are either 100 percent or 50 percent roofed. The former use bedding materials such as sawdust, straw, or wood shavings. The manure and bedding materials are removed with a metal alley scraper for land disposal. The latter, common in warmer regions, generally handle the manure as a slurry.

CAFOs have specialized equipment and technology to remove animal waste and transfer it to disposal sites. Manure storage facilities consisting of earthen basins, concrete pits, aboveground prefabricated tanks, and lagoons are used to hold manure until it is applied to the land. Settling basins allow manure solids to settle and manure liquids to drain to holding ponds or lagoons. Where the manure is in a slurry, it is moved to an outdoor holding tank or lagoon. Where mechanical scraping is used, the manure is stored in the pit or moved to a storage facility. Storing animal waste lets its disposal be coordinated with the nutrient needs of crops; the waste can thus be used as a production input.

Manure Disposal

Animal waste must be disposed of carefully to prevent pollution. Most producers take great efforts to avoid environmental contamination and use one of two application methods to convey animal waste to fields. Manure can be mixed with a dry litter for handling in a dry form, or it can be handled as a slurry and pumped into a storage facility, typically a lagoon. Waste must be stored during those periods when crops are nearing harvest or would be damaged by waste application.

Solid manure is often spread on cropland and incorporated into the soil. Waste should not be applied to frozen ground, however, if it will likely be washed into a stream or other water body. When manure is left on the surface and never incorporated into the soil, it can lose about half its total nitrogen, which either evaporates or gets washed away.[11]

Manure in semisolid (slurry) form can be injected into the soil via a mechanical process. Soil injection places the manure under the soil surface, so that the nutrients can be used by the crop, and also eliminates most of the odors associated with the application of manure to land. Recently developed injection systems spread manure in horizontal patterns under the soil surface. These systems help the manure break down more quickly and place it in a position more favorable for uptake by plants early in the growing season.

Liquids from waste lagoons are generally applied by irrigation. This method for applying large amounts of manure, although efficient, raises risks of overapplication and volatilization. Volatilization of nitrogen from liquid lagoon waste, irrigated manure, and the land application of manure causes ammonia to evaporate into the air. Gases such as ammonia, hydrogen sulfide, methane, and other organic compounds are responsible for the objectionable smells that accompany the decomposition of manure.

Antibiotics and Resistant Bacteria

The production of livestock in the United States is accompanied by the widespread use of antimicrobial drugs. In some cases producers use these drugs at low levels for therapeutic disease treatments. In other situations low levels of antimicrobial drugs improve feed efficiency and increase weight-gain rates. These drugs may also enhance carcass quality in cattle. These resulting advantages offer producers significant financial incentives to administer such drugs to their animals.

Yet their use involves risk. For one thing, bacteria may develop antimicrobial resistance, blocking the killing effects of a particular drug. Another method of control becomes necessary, generally a new antibiotic. Developing drugs is an expensive process, however. We may spend $30 billion per year due to the cumulative effects of antimicrobial resistance.[12]

Scientists have estimated that about 26.6 million pounds of antibiotics are administered to domestic livestock each year, whereas humans consume 3 million pounds.[13] Less than 8 percent of the antibiotics administered to animals are used to treat active infections.[14] The remaining quantities of drugs are intended to enhance animals' growth and producers' profits. About 70 percent of the large swine operations in the United States administer antibiotics either through injection or orally, in feed or water; for cattle, 57 percent receive antibiotics.[15]

Drugs administered to livestock help control animal infections that may be transferred to humans.[16] Given bacteria's ability to develop antimicrobial resistance, some worry that the widespread use of antibiotics in animals may exacerbate the rising incidence of such resistance in human pathogens. Experts believe that resistant strains of organisms causing illness or disease in humans (*salmonella, campylobacter,* and *E. coli*) are linked to the use of antibiotics in animals.[17] In response, scientists and governments have proposed limiting the antibiotics approved for use in livestock production.

Several European countries have already circumscribed the use of antimicrobial drugs in feed to enhance growth or feed efficiency.[18] In the United States the American Medical Association passed a resolution in 2001 opposing nontherapeutic uses of antibiotics in agriculture, and federal agencies have considered further regulation of animal antibiotics.[19]

The Department of Health and Human Services believes that the scientific evidence justifies taking steps to decrease use of antibiotics in agriculture, while the USDA believes more research is needed before implementing such regulations.[20]

The congregation of thousands of animals at confinement operations has been accompanied by increases in the use of antibiotics. Reducing the risk of disease and increasing digestive efficiency, and hence decreasing feed, are two major reasons that producers use antibiotics.[21] Large swine CAFOs are three times more likely to use antibiotics in feed and water than are small operations.[22] Large cattle operations administer antibiotics in feed and water at twice the rate of their smaller counterparts. Concentrations of animals are thus exacerbating the problem of antimicrobial resistance. Further consideration of mechanisms to guarantee the judicious use of antibiotics is needed.

Health Concerns Directly Related to CAFOs

Major health-related problems accompany the production of animals at CAFOs. It's difficult to say whether animal waste impairs humans' health, however; information on quantities of particular pathogens or excess nutrients is too scant for us to know what can be attributed to animal operations. Nevertheless, infected animals can excrete pathogens that may survive for some time in animal waste, and research has shown that pathogenic microbes in animal waste can infect people.[23] Outbreaks of cryptosporidiosis in England and Scotland were attributed to animal waste.[24] *Giardia* cysts have survived up to thirty-three days in animal waste. *Salmonella* contained in animal waste can survive up to three weeks on vegetation, thirty-six months in feces, and over two years in soil. Because CAFOs may adversely affect human health, citizens and legislators are taking a more active role in advocating controls and requirements to help protect the public.

Harm from Nutrients

CAFOs produce potentially harmful concentrations of nitrogen and phosphorus, and other nutrients are being scrutinized as well. The dangers of heavy metals in swine manure have led South Carolina to set annual constituent loading rates for copper and zinc. The accumulation of excessive amounts of arsenic also provokes concern, which has led to regulations of arsenic levels in liquid animal waste.

In addition, manure contains nitrates, which may endanger human health when elevated levels are present in drinking water. The intensive application of manure can increase this risk. Excessive nitrates are particularly problematic for infants. Ingested nitrate is transformed into nitrite; the resultant diminished oxygen transport-transfer capability means the child has less oxygen in its blood (anoxia), a condition indicated by cyanosis, the bluish skin tone seen in "blue-baby syndrome."[25]

Excessive amounts of nitrates can harm livestock as well. Research by the Centers for Disease Control suggests a relationship between nitrates and abortions in laboratory animals and livestock.[26] Other reports suggest that nitrates converted to nitrites can be toxic to livestock.[27]

Pathogens

Animal waste present three sorts of pathogens that have the potential to harm humans: viruses, bacteria, and parasites. Research suggests that this waste may contain hepatitis E viruses, reoviruses, rotaviruses, adenoviruses, caliciviruses, and influenza viruses.[28] The bacteria may include *Salmonella ssp., Campylobacter spp., Escherichia coli, Aeromonas hydrophila, Yersinia enterocolitica, Vibrio spp., Leptospira spp.,* and *Listeria spp.* The parasites may include *Cryptosporidium parvum, Giardia lamblia,* and *Balantidium coli.*

Microbial water contamination and disease transmission also demand consideration. Since manure slurries can propagate *E. coli* and other pathogens, irrigating land with them endangers both human and animal health.[29] Nor is land application of manure without risk, for even modest rainfalls can move fecal coliforms into soil and water supplies.

Animal-waste-borne pathogens in our water constitute an unacceptable health risk. Americans want and expect safe water supplies, and they are beginning to ask for governmental guarantees that livestock production not foul our waters. State legislators and agencies have responded with new state laws and regulations that place more controls over the pollutants released by AFOs. Moreover, using environmental groups such as the Waterkeeper Alliance[30] and the Sierra Club,[31] citizens have been active in publicizing pollution events and bringing lawsuits for some of the more egregious pollution problems.[32]

Other Afflictions

An additional problem involves the increased risk of chronic respiratory diseases associated with swine confinement operations. The Centers for Disease Control and the National Center for Environmental Health list numerous studies documenting environment-related health problems among swine confinement workers.[33] Persons living next to CAFOs, as well as those working in buildings with animal manure, have reported problems such as respiratory irritation, headaches, diarrhea, and sore throats.[34] Odorous emissions from animal facilities can induce eye irritation, nausea, coughs, stress, and mood alterations.[35]

Animal waste has been mentioned in conjunction with several notable pollution incidents. Various news reports have blamed animal waste for outbreaks of *Pfiesteria* in Chesapeake Bay tributaries,[36] fish kills in North Carolina,[37] a cryptosporidiosis epidemic in Milwaukee's water supply,[38] and deaths from *E. coli* in a Canadian public water supply.[39] Although not all these charges have been proved, evidence does show animal waste contaminating water supplies.

Finally, even greater concerns exist about bovine spongiform encephalopathy (BSE—also known as "mad cow" disease) and foot-and-mouth disease. BSE, which can be fatal in humans, has been linked to the use of ruminant carcasses and offal in animal feed. Although the federal government has banned this practice, further enforcement of the ban may be advisable.[40] Because foot-and-mouth disease can markedly increase animal-production costs, we will take extraordinary efforts to prevent its introduction into our country. Fears that citizens or animals could be exposed to either of these diseases suggest that governments need to be vigilant in devising appropriate responses.

Animal Welfare

Some critics have also expressed concern over the welfare of animals produced in industrialized operations. Many object to their confinement without social contact. Others object to the use of animals for experimentation. Numerous groups have claimed that changes occurring in the production of animals threaten the well-being of humanity.[41] Some European countries have restricted the use of animals for research, outlawed the production of animals for fur, and banned extreme confinement situations. Groups in the United States are calling for legislation eliminating the use of animals for research and for the elimination of certain confinement practices. Other issues include animal cruelty in circuses, rodeos, and other settings.

Ethics demands that we avoid inflicting pain or other harm to animals. But further issues demand consideration as well; we may ask, for example, how animal production should take place, whether we should be allowed to genetically manipulate animals, and what duties (if any) we owe to animals. One central issue arises from the suffering of the 25 million vertebrate animals our nation's laboratories currently hold for purposes including biomedical research; drug, vaccine, and consumer products testing; and education. Groups such as the Humane Society of the United States promote nonanimal research methods to reduce and eliminate harm to animals, such as forgoing the use of mice for producing monoclonal antibodies.

Other groups have more focused goals. People for the Ethical Treatment of Animals has been quite successful in bringing examples of animal mistreatment before the public and forcing corporations to alter practices. McDonald's, Burger King, and Wendy's have ended certain practices following intense pressure from this animal-rights group.[42] (It is perhaps ironic that the colossal McDonald's restaurant chain has been a player in opposing factory farming.)[43]

More serious concerns exist about genetically modifying animals, for not all changes are advantageous or neutral; some are deleterious. For example, genetic modifications for studying a disease can yield unintended negative effects (such as the development of tumors) that cause the animals to suffer. The animals' rights may come into play as well, as in genetic manipulation to produce organs for transplants into humans, which presents a dramatic example of using animals solely as objects for human benefit. This concern also explains some people's objection to cloning, with the claim being that it demeans animals as being entities of purely functional worth.

For CAFOs the question is not whether producers are treating their animals cruelly but whether the animals are suffering. Three production procedures suggest that they do suffer excessively. First, diets (for veal calves) and crowded conditions may exacerbate diseases. Second, the lack of individual attention to animals may mean that a producer is oblivious to an injured animal. Third, the physical and psychological deprivation associated with confinement may harm animals. These conditions have caused some to argue for a new code of ethics to address the welfare of confined animals. Florida amended the state constitution to ban the caging of pregnant sows.[44]

New legislation forbidding practices may well emerge, but a more likely response will stem from consumer movements toward "greener" crops, including livestock. Products are now available bearing the American Humane Association's "free-farmed" certification, which requires, among other things, that the animals receive all-natural, antibiotic-free feed.[45] Similar standards are prescribed by the British Royal Society for the

Prevention of Cruelty to Animals. Although antibiotics are allowed for disease treatment for individual animals, subtherapeutic antibiotics and mammalian-derived protein are prohibited.[46] Other regulations cover items such as castration, tail docking, weaning, and housing conditions.

New Approaches to Animal Pollution

Pollution from agriculture is not a new concern. In fact, agricultural researchers have been addressing it for some time. The question is how best to reduce it, whether through new technology or through improved approaches to pollution management.

Looking back to the National Symposium on Animal Waste Management that highlighted the animal-waste issues of the 1960s,[47] we discover objectives that remain valid today. We need to delineate the problems of managing animal waste so as to discern the obstacles to ending pollution. We need to evaluate current and potential technologies for handling waste. What superior measures or technologies are our researchers and scientists advancing? Can we give new direction to employing technology to end contamination and other problems? How can we develop a regulatory structure that uses science to respond to these problems?

The symposium admonished us to examine the big picture. Its epilogue suggested using an overall systems approach considering costs and benefits, aesthetics, social issues, the total environment, and legal parameters. We have not successfully responded to this challenge. Although scientists at land-grant universities have made impressive strides in developing new technologies, and producers have garnered impressive efficiency gains, we have not adequately considered legal and social alternatives. Our regulatory framework has not kept pace with scientific advancements. Despite the landmark environmental and social legislation of the 1960s and 1970s, and experiences in the implementation of their provisions, many regulations are antiquated, ineffective, and inefficient.

We have spent billions of dollars on temporary solutions to the exclusion of more permanent improvements. We seek to hold producers accountable for by-products polluting our soils and streams but fail to devise methods to reward those who provide public goods by preserving habitats or providing scenic landscapes. We offer financial support for the adoption of conservation practices while failing to compensate those landowners already practicing conservation. More problematic, legislatures and regulators have failed to enforce existing regulations. Since regulatory budgets often go underfunded, laws are often unenforced, leading to shirkers. These observations disclose opportunities for revising our regulatory framework to more meaningfully respond to environmental and societal objectives.

NOTES

1. U.S. Department of Agriculture, *Agricultural Statistics 2001* (Washington, D.C.: USDA, 2001), VI-18, VIII-31, VIII-40, VIII-43, VIII-47.
2. Arkansas Public Policy Panel, "Changes in Arkansas Agriculture February 18, 1999" (available at <http://arpanel.org/studies/farmstats/>), table 1.
3. Texas Agricultural Statistics Service, "Texas Cattle Operations by Size" (available at <http://www.io.com/tass/lvstkgif.htm>), 1999.
4. "Animal Factories: Pollution and Health Threats to Rural Texas," *Consumers Union,* May 2000, p. 2.
5. Natural Resources Defense Council, *America's Animal Factories,* ch. 17.
6. Marla Cone, "State Dairy Farms Try to Clean Up Their Act," *Los Angeles Times,* Apr. 28, 1998, p. A1.
7. National Council for Science and the Environment, *Animal Waste Management and the Environment: Background for Current Issues Environment: Waste from Animal Agriculture,* no. 98-451 (Washington, D.C.: Congressional Research Service, 1998).
8. Environmental Protection Agency, *Preliminary Data Summary: Feedlots Point Source Category Study,* EPA-821-R-99-002 (Washington, D.C.: Office of Water, 1999), 14.
9. Ibid.
10. Susan Pollack, "Holding the World at Bay," *Sierra,* May–June 1996, pp. 50–59.
11. Michael Schmitt and George Rehm, *Fertilizing Cropland with Dairy Manure* (St. Paul: University of Minnesota Extension Service, 1999).
12. American College of Physicians-American Society of Internal Medicine, "Emerging Antimicrobial Resistance Facts and Figures" (available at <http://www.acponline.org/ear/factsfigs.htm>).
13. Jane E. Brody, "Studies Find Resistant Bacteria in Meats," *New York Times,* Oct. 18, 2001, p. A12.
14. Ibid.
15. Animal and Plant Health Inspection Service, *Antimicrobial Resistance Issues in Animal Agriculture* (Washington, D.C.: U.S. Department of Agriculture, 1999), 24.
16. Ibid., 17.
17. General Accounting Office, *Food Safety: The Agricultural Use of Antibiotics and Its Implications for Human Health,* GAO/RCED-99-74 (Washington, D.C.: GAO, 1999), 4.
18. Kenneth H. Matthews Jr., *Antimicrobial Resistance and Veterinary Costs in U.S. Livestock Production* (Washington, D.C.: U.S. Department of Agriculture, 2000), 3.
19. Robbin Marks, *Cesspools of Shame: How Factory Farm Lagoons and Sprayfields Threaten Environmental and Public Health* (Washington, D.C.: Natural Resources Defense Council and Clean Water Network, 2001), 24.

20. General Accounting Office, *Food Safety*, 2.

21. Animal and Plant Health Inspection Service, *Antimicrobial Resistance*, 18.

22. Ibid., 24.

23. Marks, *Cesspools of Shame*, 21.

24. P. S. Hooda, A. C. Edwards, H. A. Anderson, and A. Miller, "A Review of Water Quality Concerns in Livestock Farming Areas," *The Science of the Total Environment* 250 (2000): 143–67.

25. Larry W. Canter, *Nitrates in Groundwater* (Boca Raton: Lewis, 1997), 15.

26. Centers for Disease Control, "Spontaneous Abortions Possibly Related to Ingestion of Nitrate-Contaminated Well Water—LaGrange County, Indiana, 1991–1994," *Morbidity and Mortality Weekly Report* 45 (1996): 569–72

27. Margaret Rosso Grossman, "Nitrates from Agriculture in Europe: The EC Nitrates Directive and Its Implementation in England," *Boston College Environmental Affairs Law Review* 27 (2000): 567–629.

28. M. D. Sobsey, L. A. Khatib, V. R. Hill, E. Alocilja and S. Pillai, *Pathogens in Animal Wastes and the Impacts of Waste Management Practices on their Survival, Transport and Fate*, White Papers on Animal Agriculture and the Environment (Raleigh, N.C.: National Center for Manure and Animal Waste Management, 2001), 54–57.

29. I. T. Kudva, K. Blanch, and C. J. Hovde, "Analysis of *Escherichia coli* O157:H7 Survival in Ovine or Bovine Manure and Manure Slurry," *Applied and Environmental Microbiology* 64 (1998): 3166–74.

30. Water Keeper Alliance, Inc. v. Smithfield Foods, Inc., 53 Env't Rep. Cas. (BNA) 1506; 32 ELR 20320 (2001).

31. Ken Midkiff, "Taking Big Pig to Court, *The Planet Newsletter* (available at <http://www.sierraclub.org/planet/200110/pig.asp>), Oct. 2001.

32. Community Association for Restoration of the Environment v. Henry Bosma Dairy, 65 F. Supp. 2d 1129, 1133 (E.D. Wash. 1999); Community Association for Restoration of the Environment v. Sid Koopman Dairy, 54 F. Supp. 2d 976, 981 (E.D. Wash. 1999).

33. Centers for Disease Control and Prevention and National Center for Environmental Health, *The Confinement Animal Feeding Operation Workshop* (Washington, D.C.: National Center for Environmental Health, 1998).

34. "Animal Factories: Pollution and Health Threats to Rural Texas," *Consumers Union SWRO* (May 2000).

35. S. S. Schiffman, B. B. Auverman, and R. W. Bottcher, *Health Effects of Aerial Emissions from Animal Production and Waste Management Systems*, White Papers on Animal Agriculture and the Environment (Raleigh, N.C.: National Center for Manure and Animal Waste Management, 2002), ch. 4.

36. John P. Almeida, "Nonpoint Source Pollution and Chesapeake Bay Pfiesteria Blooms: The Chickens Come Home to Roost," *Georgia Law Review* 32 (1998): 1195–1225.

37. Ronald Smothers, "Spill Puts a Spotlight on a Powerful Industry," *New York Times*, June 30, 1995, p. A10.

38. Marilynn Marchione, "Judge Reduces Crypto Claims against City," *Milwaukee Journal Sentinel*, March 14, 1998, p. 1.

39. M. A. J. McKenna, "*E. Coli* Danger High for Months? Ontario Town Battling Bacteria, Fear," *Atlanta Constitution*, May 30, 2000, p. A1.

40. Minnesota Environmental Quality Board, *Generic Environmental Impact Statement on Animal Agriculture* (Minneapolis: State of Minnesota, July 2002), appendix D, 315.

41. John Hodges, "Why Livestock, Ethics, and Quality of Life?" in *Livestock Ethics and Quality of Life,* ed. John Hodges and In K. Han (New York: CABI, 1999), 1–26.

42. Bruce Horowitz, "Wendy's Steps up Animal Welfare Standards," *USA Today,* Sept. 6, 2001, p. 2B.

43. Laurent Belsie, "Chicken Tenderly," *Christian Science Monitor,* Nov. 6, 2000.

44. Associated Press, "Pregnant Pigs Get Constitutional Protection," wire service story, Nov. 5, 2002.

45. "Du Breton Natural Pork Earns Animal Welfare Certification," *National Hog Farmer,* May 15, 2001.

46. Ibid.

47. E. Paul Taiganides, "Symposium Prologue," in *American Society of Agricultural Engineers, Management of Farm Animal Wastes, National Symposium on Animal Waste Management,* SP-0366 (1966), 1.

4 Concentrations of Animals and Water Pollution

Canadaway Creek was both a diversion and a bane. The power of its unruly flow, occasional floods, and ice jams awed me as an impressionable youngster. But more sinister was its pollution. Canadaway Creek traversed the neighboring village, which elected to place its only sewage facility on the waterway. In the 1960s the creek served as the village's conduit for dispersing partially treated human waste.

In all fairness, I should add that a population explosion had caught this village by surprise. Similar situations existed in hundreds of other municipalities all over the country. The village was unable to plan for and fund the expansion of its sewage-treatment plant in a timely fashion. In addition, the facility undoubtedly lacked adequate secondary treatment equipment. We did not yet have the Clean Water Act or federal grants for funding sewage-treatment plants. As a result, the plant never had the capacity to handle the waste generated by the village. Because of the partially treated waste, the creek offended both the eye and the nose, with a conspicuous, smelly sludge amassing in the pools, among the rocks, and on the gravel creekbed.

My most vivid memories of the creek come from the summer. Seeking distraction, my siblings and I would explore every corner of our farm, and one activity was to cross the creek while wearing gym shoes. This involved finding somewhere you could step from one large stone to another. The game was great fun, especially since any misstep involved abhorrent consequences. A slip from a rock into the creek meant that a detestable scum of partially treated sewage would envelop your foot. The unlucky person was left to devise a strategy to clean the evidence or respond to a subsequent parental admonition.

Canadaway Creek's story is typical, for the same thing has occurred in rivers and other water bodies throughout the world. Water has historically served as a conduit for the disposal of refuse, including human and animal waste and by-products discharged from factories. In the United States point-source pollutants were commonly deposited into waters and onto land until the enactment of environmental controls during the late 1960s and the 1970s. Waters near most populated areas were horribly polluted. Even Lake Erie, with its expansive waters to absorb contaminants, was so polluted that it suffered summer fish kills and its beaches had to be closed to swimming.

Governmental regulations have reduced water pollution, but contamination problems remain. We are still attempting to meet water-quality goals set thirty years ago. Our major focus has been on pollutants from point sources, such as factories, municipal treatment plants, and other identifiable entities. Success at eliminating pollution from such facilities, however, has revealed agriculture to be a major source of pollution; AFOs, and especially CAFOs, have been major components of the pollution from this sphere.

Water Pollutants from AFOs

By its nature animal production tends to create pollutants. Animals generate waste, which can pollute the areas used for its disposal. Such pollution often comes with offensive smells and even health problems. In addition, manure applied to the land can introduce particulates, nutrients, and bacteria into the environment. Rains can carry these components

into streams and other bodies of water. Especially problematic are phosphorus and nitrogen, the two major nutrients that contribute to the
eutrophication of water bodies.

Pollution from animal production has become more conspicuous as
animals have become increasingly concentrated at production facilities
and in regions. An estimated 9 percent of our nation's impaired river and
stream miles have contaminants from animal feedlots.[1] When animals
were raised on many farms and their manure was used as fertilizer, streams
and water bodies usually were not overwhelmed by the animal-waste
pollutants, but the concentration of animals has increased the potential
for pollution.

To reduce transportation and other costs, AFOs often dispose of manure quickly and as close as possible to the facility where it was generated.[2]
Disposal is generally accomplished by land application—machinery carries the manure from holding facilities and deposits it on nearby fields and
pastures. Producers may apply manure as a fertilizer, but large amounts
and multiple applications may result in excessive quantities in given
fields. Research shows excessive quantities of phosphorus are more prevalent on lands receiving manure from CAFOs than on lands receiving
manure from small operators.[3]

Federal Regulation of CAFOs

Governments have recognized that, given their size, CAFOs are more
likely to pollute than are smaller operations. Legislation therefore differ-
entiates AFOs according to size, and large AFOs meeting the legislative
definition of a CAFO are classified as point sources of pollutants. Once an
AFO is classified as a CAFO, it must obtain either a federal National Pollutant Discharge Elimination System (NPDES) permit or a similar permit
issued by a state authorized to issue state permits.[4] Non-CAFOs are not
required to have a federal permit, although a state may impose its own
permit requirements. The federal government has special effluent guidelines for CAFOs governing manure, litter, and wastewater discharges.
Separate provisions exist in four categories of animals: (1) horses and
sheep; (2) ducks; (3) dairy cows and cattle other than veal calves; and (4)
swine, poultry other than ducks, and veal calves.[5]

For approximately twenty-five years established federal regulations
determined whether a farm or ranch raising animals was a CAFO. In December 2002 the Environmental Protection Agency (EPA) revised these
regulations to augment governmental oversight of potential pollution

sources. Although the revised regulations largely retained the previous classification system, they established further requirements to safeguard water quality. The new regulations also expanded the scope of federal control to cover greater numbers of AFOs.

Defining an AFO

To determine whether a facility constitutes an AFO, we look for the confinement of domestic animals. For facilities that keep animals in pens or cages, the answer is obvious: they are AFOs. For facilities that have animals in barns or limited encumbered areas, we must look further. To earn the AFO designation, the animal-production facility must confine and feed animals for a total of forty-five days or more during any twelve-month period.[6] In addition, the animals must prevent vegetative forage growth from surviving the normal growing season over a portion of the confined area. Production facilities that do not meet one of these requirements are not AFOs.

Feedlots and dairies are AFOs. Most livestock farms that enclose and feed animals until they are ready for sale are AFOs. Stockyards, auction barns, pens, corrals, roundup areas, and wintering facilities may be AFOs. Ranches with thousands of cattle that graze in pastures or on the range are not AFOs, however—the animals are not confined in a limited area.

Numbers of Animals for a CAFO

Similarly, an AFO must meet certain criteria to count as a CAFO, a category with three subtypes determined by the production and dissemination of pollutants and the number of animals of any one species: large, medium, and small CAFOs.

Since different species raise different issues, the EPA determined threshold numbers of different animal species to be used in designating large and medium CAFOs. The following list shows the numbers of animals that qualify an operation as a large CAFO:

—700 mature dairy cows, whether milked or dry
—1,000 veal calves
—1,000 cattle other than mature dairy cows or veal calves (This category includes but is not limited to heifers, steers, bulls and cow-calf pairs.)
—2,500 swine, each weighing 55 pounds or more
—10,000 swine, each weighing less than 55 pounds
—500 horses

—10,000 sheep or lambs

—55,000 turkeys

—30,000 laying hens or broilers if the AFO uses a liquid-manure-handling system

—125,000 chickens (other than laying hens) if the AFO uses other than a liquid-manure-handling system

—82,000 laying hens if the AFO uses other than a liquid-manure-handling system;

—30,000 ducks if the AFO uses other than a liquid-manure-handling system

—5,000 ducks if the AFO uses a liquid-manure-handling system[7]

Medium CAFOs house fewer animals than do large CAFOs and involve a discharge of pollutants. For example, a medium CAFO may have 200 to 699 mature dairy cattle; 300 to 999 cattle other than mature dairy cows or veal calves; or 750 to 2,499 swine, each weighing 55 pounds or more. In addition, a medium CAFO must either (1) discharge pollutants directly into waters or (2) allow pollutants to be discharged directly into waters that pass through the facility or come into contact with animals confined at the facility.

Designated CAFOs

Federal regulators realized that numbers of animals should not be the only criteria used to determine whether we should require an AFO to secure an NPDES permit. The federal regulations thus allow authorized governmental officials to designate small CAFOs.[8] A small CAFO need not have a threshold number of animals. Instead, it receives this designation if an on-site inspection shows it to be impairing water quality. Few AFOs have been designated under this authority, but it offers an important avenue to respond to problematic situations. Moreover, citizens might demand that this designation be used more in the future.

Designation authority resides with the state director of an authorized permit program and the EPA regional administrator. To designate a small CAFO in a state with an approved state program, the regional administrator must determine that at least one pollutant is being discharged into waters in common use.

The regulations list several factors for consideration. First, the designator can evaluate the size of the AFO, because larger facilities are more likely to threaten water quality. Second, the AFO's location is important. The closer the AFO is to waters, the more likely it is to present a problem.

Third, regulators must look at the means by which process wastewater and animal waste are conveyed into waters, evaluating the natural and man-made structures that carry the waste to determine whether the facility is likely to contribute significantly to water pollution—as can happen if, say, animals have direct contact with surface waters.

Finally, regulators can consider topographic or climatic features affecting the likelihood or frequency of discharge of animal waste and process wastewaters into waters. Making this determination involves considering several factors, including the slope of the feedlot and surrounding land, the feedlot surface, rainfall, soil type, groundwater depth, drainage and storage structures, buffers, and runoff volume.

Mandatory Permits

Any AFO that meets the CAFO criteria must have an NPDES or similar state permit. Given the regulations adopted in December 2002, this means that approximately 15,500 operations should qualify as CAFOs and thus need permits. Only about 4,500 AFOs have been issued permits, however, whether by the federal government or by a state-level agency. Confused by the previously operative criteria, some regulators have been lax in requiring CAFOs to secure permits. In addition, state regulators sometimes seek to avoid inconveniencing farmers or offending state legislators. Facing powerful agricultural interests, limited agency budgets, and a lack of resources to monitor AFOs, governments have not actively sought to monitor compliance.

Even when this inaction reflects the best motives—an attempt, say, not to burden farmers—state agencies' failures to step in can prove counterproductive. For example, by failing to enforce current regulations, regulators allow streams, rivers, and lakes to become polluted. The Clean Water Act, however, requires that polluted bodies of water be listed, which means that the state must develop a total maximum daily load (TMDL) program. Thus, lax regulatory oversight of pollution from CAFOs may lead to additional expenses in meeting TMDL requirements. Furthermore, failure to control CAFO pollution encourages the public and legislators to request even more stringent regulations.

The NPDES permit system stipulates conditions governing CAFOs to ensure the attainment of applicable state-established water-quality standards. Where states have not adopted water-quality standards, regulators can implement response actions to address pollution problems. In addition, a state may adopt controls more stringent than those required by the

Clean Water Act. Twenty-five states have permit programs that incorporate some other state permit, license, or authorization program for CAFOs,[9] which indicates widespread interest in curtailing pollution from animal operations.

Nutrient-Management Plans

A major method for addressing animal-waste pollution is to require AFOs to develop and implement nutrient-management plans. Such plans are especially important for CAFOs with significant manure production, unacceptable conditions, and practices likely to impair water quality, and comprehensive nutrient-management plans have been obligatory for all CAFOs. AFO operators, too, have developed such plans, building on the ethic of land stewardship and sustainability. Their importance in reducing nutrient pollution has led one state to recommend that every facility with more than fifty cows (or a comparable number of animals of another species) have a management plan.[10]

The AFO operator is responsible for developing and implementing a nutrient-management plan. Technical assistance for developing comprehensive plans is available from federal agencies including the Natural Resources Conservation Service, Cooperative Extension Service agents and specialists, soil and water conservation districts, and land-grant universities. Operators can also receive assistance from private consultants, integrators, industry associations, and qualified vendors. The USDA's *Natural Resources Conservation Service Field Office Technical Guide* is the primary technical reference for the development of comprehensive nutrient-management plans.

The new federal regulations require every CAFO to formulate a nutrient-management plan. States may elect to continue their own comprehensive management-plan requirements as long as they meet federal requirements.

Effluent-Limitations Guidelines

CAFOs with manure, litter, or process wastewater discharges are also governed by effluent-limitations guidelines that place additional requirements on nutrient-management plans.[11] Large CAFOs raising dairy cows, cattle, swine, poultry, and veal calves are required to develop and implement best management practices for the land application of manure, litter, and process wastewater consisting of a nutrient-management plan, waste-application rates, manure and soil sampling, inspection for leaks, and setbacks.[12] Other provisions delineate distinctive technological requirements for CAFO production areas, CAFO land-application areas, and new sources. While the effluent-limitations guidelines' land-application requirements apply only to some large CAFOs, other CAFOs are subject to the provisions on land-application discharges through the NPDES permit requirements.[13]

Large CAFOs with animals in the previously mentioned categories must file a nutrient-management plan based on a field-specific assessment of the potential for nitrogen and phosphorus transport. Application rates for manure, litter, and process wastewater must minimize the movement of nitrogen and phosphorus from the field to surface waters. Annual analyses of manure are required for nitrogen and phosphorus content. Soils must be analyzed at least once every five years for phosphorus content. Under best management practices, nutrients will end up nourishing crops rather than being carried into surface waters.

Another significant provision specifies setback requirements for the applications of manure, litter, and process wastewater. Applications cannot be made within one hundred feet of any down-gradient surface waters, open tile-line intake structures, sinkholes, agricultural wellheads, or other conduits to surface waters. However, since this requirement would be overly restrictive in some situations, a CAFO may select an alternative compliance measure using a thirty-five-foot vegetated buffer where there is no application of manure, litter, or process wastewater. Moreover, a CAFO may demonstrate to the permitting authority that a setback or vegetated buffer is unnecessary or may be reduced.

Most large CAFOs must take several additional measures. Each week the owner or operator must visually inspect all storm-water diversion devices, runoff diversion structures, animal-waste storage structures, and devices channeling contaminated storm water to storage and containment structures. Daily inspections of water lines, including those for drinking or cooling water, should be performed. Existing operations with liquid impoundments must use depth markers to indicate the design volume and to clearly indicate the minimum capacity necessary to contain a twenty-five-year, twenty-four-hour rainfall event. Any deficiency discovered during these inspections must be remedied as soon as possible.

Production and Application Areas

Most CAFOs—probably 90 percent—will dispose of animal waste through a land-application method, a preferred technique because it reuses the nitrogen and phosphorus for crop production. The federal permit requirements apply with respect to all animals in confinement at a CAFO and all manure, litter, and process wastewater generated by those animals or their production. Federal regulations thus govern both production areas and lands used for the application of CAFO by-products.

Production areas are defined to include animal-confinement areas, manure-storage areas, raw-materials-storage areas, and waste-containment areas.[14] Further provisions define each of these four areas, all of which are distinguished from land-application areas.

A land-application area is defined as "land under the control of an AFO owner or operator, whether it is owned, rented, or leased, to which manure, litter or process wastewater from the production area is or may be applied." CAFO regulations go on to stipulate requirements for land-application discharges, unless they qualify as an agricultural storm-water discharge.

Agricultural Storm-Water Discharges

The Clean Water Act exempts agricultural storm-water discharges from its point-source regulations.[15] Producers have interpreted this longstanding exemption to mean that runoff from the application of manure cannot be regulated under the CAFO regulations. The revised federal regulations resolve this issue by differentiating two types of land-application discharges: agricultural storm-water discharges that continue to qualify under the existing exemption and other discharges subject to the NPDES permit requirements.[16]

Discharges stemming from a rainfall event when manure, litter, or process wastewater was applied in accordance with site-specific nutrient-management practices are classed as agricultural storm-water discharges. In these situations, the producer has applied the manure so as to ensure appropriate agricultural utilization of the nutrients as a production input. Such discharges fall outside regulatory oversight under the agricultural storm-water discharge exemption.

However, any such discharge that occurs because manure and process wastewater were misapplied according to the previously mentioned criterion does not count as an agricultural storm-water discharge and thus falls under the CAFO regulations. Moreover, any discharge occurring without a rain event is not a agricultural storm-water discharge.

Co-permitting

Public concern about contamination from manure and abandoned production facilities has led to proposals for additional regulatory requirements to safeguard our environment. Believing that some producers can't afford to ameliorate the problems their operations create, regulators are seeking backup sources of financial responsibility, and integration within the poultry and pork industries has made integrators reasonable candidates. Given the low profit margins and adhesive contracts typical for producers in these industries, it makes sense to hold integrators (including processing companies) liable for waste-disposal expenses related to animal production. This has become known as "co-permitting."

Under a co-permitting system, owners and operators of AFOs above a certain size must obtain a permit. This includes persons who direct the manner in which the animals will be housed or fed and persons who control the inputs or other material aspects of the CAFO. Integrators and processors thus fall within this category and can incur liability for problems associated with the AFO.

Although not implementing co-permitting requirements across the board, Maryland requires its poultry companies to obtain a Poultry Processor Discharge permit.[17] This system requires poultry processors to ensure that contract growers have nutrient-management plans and dispose of poultry litter properly.

Co-permitting regulations are not economically justifiable in a competitive market.[18] Conversely, where producers have little opportunity for marketing with a firm other than an integrator, the co-permitting regulations may constitute a positive environmental development.

Co-permitting requirements were not included in the new federal regulations, and Kentucky has taken action to negate its co-permitting provisions. Although laws addressing hazardous waste show that legislative bodies can hold related individuals and businesses liable for the activities of others, the problems accompanying improper disposal of animal waste do not appear to be that egregious. There are better ways to deal with the issue.

Alternative Responses

Do the revised federal CAFO regulations respond effectively to existing point-source pollution problems? Perhaps not; although the regulations bring more AFOs under regulatory controls and enact further measures to intercept potential pollutants, we may need additional steps to prevent AFOs from shunting contaminants into water bodies and the air.

Experts have noted a number of shortcomings. Above all, we will not solve the problem of excess nutrients solely by regulating CAFOs; agricultural fertilizers, animals not raised at CAFOs, urban runoff, and residential uses of commercial fertilizers must share some of the blame. We might start with attempting to devise ways to determine the origins of particular pollutants rather than proceeding with blanket regulations for additional CAFOs. Alternatively, our governmental oversight of animals might consider animal density.

In addition, current and proposed CAFO regulations fail to consider phosphorus excretion, which might be a more appropriate way to regulate water pollution from animal waste. Although the revised regulations require CAFOs' nutrient-management plans to consider phosphorus transport from fields to waters, this nutrient plays no direct role in a CAFO classification.For measuring environmental risk, however, the production of phosphorus in a watershed or region may be more important than the numbers of animals owned by any one operator.

Furthermore, both existing and proposed rules ignore animal housing and manure containment in specifying criteria for CAFO status, even though these features may be more important than numbers and species. A CAFO with roofed housing is much less likely to create an environmental problem than one with unroofed housing. CAFOs that store manure during periods when it should not be applied to land might be governed by different regulations. Rather than impose requirements solely on the basis of livestock numbers, the rules could differentiate based on manure-management distinctions related to the potential for water impairment. Moderate-sized AFOs employing good practices might qualify for an exemption from CAFO requirements.

NOTES

1. General Accounting Office, *Animal Agriculture: Information on Waste Management and Water Quality Issues,* GAO/RCED-95-200BR (Washington, D.C.: GAO, 1995), 6.

2. Laura L. Jackson, "Restoring Prairie Processes to Farmlands," in *The Farm as a Natural Habitat: Reconnecting Food Systems with Ecosystems,* ed. Dana L. Jackson and Laura L. Jackson (Washington, D.C.: Island, 2002), 148.

3. Ibid.

4. Environmental Protection Agency, *Preliminary Data Summary: Feedlots Point Source Category Study,* EPA-821-R-99-002 (Washington, D.C.: Office of Water, 1999), 2.

5. *Code of Federal Regulations,* title 40, pt. 412.

6. Ibid., §122.23(b)(1).

7. Ibid., §122.23(b)(4).

8. Ibid., §122.23(c).

9. Environmental Protection Agency, *State Compendium: Programs and Regulatory Activities Related to Animal Feeding Operations* (Washington, D.C.: EPA, 2001), 5.

10. Minnesota Environmental Quality Board, *Generic Environmental Impact Statement on Animal Agriculture* (St. Paul: Minnesota Environmental Quality Board, 2002), app. D, 319.

11. *Code of Federal Regulations,* title 40, pt. 412.

12. Ibid., §412.4(c).

13. Ibid., §122.23(e).

14. Ibid., §§122.23(b)(8) and 412.2(h).

15. *U.S. Code Annotated,* title 30, §1362(14) (2002).

16. *Code of Federal Regulations,* title 40, §122.23(e).

17. Maryland Department of the Environment, "Department Moves Ahead with Poultry Integrator Permit," *MD Environment* 5, no. 4 (Aug. 2001): 4, 12.

18. Tomislav Vukina, *The Relationship between Contracting and Livestock Waste Pollution,* National Center for Manure and Animal Waste Management White Papers (Raleigh, N.C.: National Center for Manure and Animal Waste Management, 2002), ch. 18.

5   State AFO Regulations

*A*lthough I was young then, I remember the "good old days" of milk cans and delivery. The cans were kept in the milk cooler—a refrigerated tank of water that chilled the warm cow's milk. Milk cans remained in the cooler one or two days, until they were delivered to a processing plant. Dad delivered the milk to the processing plant six days a week. He had a pulley to raise the heavy cans from the cooler, move them away, and lower them to the concrete floor. Each can was rolled on its bottom rim to the pickup truck and lifted onto the back. Some days in the late spring, when he wanted more time for outdoor jobs, Dad would deliver the milk right after breakfast. My siblings and I would hop into the truck, and he would take us to our elementary school. After dropping us off, Dad would continue another half-mile to the processing plant. He must have maintained an exact schedule, for I cannot remember ever being early or late for school.

My best memory of milk cans, however, came from accompanying Dad to the processing plant on Saturdays or during a vacation. Sometimes I walked into the plant, and an employee would give me a half-pint of chocolate milk. This was a real treat, since we did not buy chocolate syrup and always drank our own, plain milk.

Nevertheless, one day Dad announced that the processing plant would no longer accept milk cans—mechanization was leading to a new system of milk transport. We had to remodel the barn and install a bulk tank. Our milk would be picked up every other day by a milk hauler with a tanker. As is commonly recognized, bulk tanks provide a fresher and safer milk supply than does transport via milk cans. The electrically cooled tanks would bring the warm cow's milk to a suitable holding temperature more quickly. This progress meant physical changes in the milk house and to the yard.

For health reasons, the bulk tank had to be in a room separated from all other activities. This isolated the tank from the odors, insects, and grime of the barn and from vehicles. We poured a cement floor and built walls for the new room. Next, a new stainless steel bulk tank was hauled in and installed. It was awesome, so modern and shiny. Out in the yard, we imported loads of gravel for a new driveway. The bulk tanker had to be able to park within feet of the tank so we could pump the milk via a short hose from the tank to the tanker. We had to keep adding gravel the first two years, because the tanker kept pushing it down into the clayey soil underneath.

Public-health objectives underlie numerous governmental regulations. As new technology (such as a bulk tank) becomes available, the government may adopt new requirements. Similarly, scientific discoveries may lead to safer procedures or products. State and local governments have broad powers for dealing with public-health, safety, and environmental issues. Given the health and environmental concerns accompanying animal production, state governments have been active in regulating AFOs. For example, under the authority of the federal Clean Water Act, every state has designated a lead state agency to respond to water pollutants from AFOs. (See appendix 1 for a list of agencies regulating CAFOs.)[1]

This decentralized approach lets any one state learn from others that have instituted regulations, policies, and programs more adept in responding to animal-waste problems. Armed with information about measures taken in other states, citizens can advocate additional provisions for addressing pollution problems in their own. Furthermore, county or local governments may seek to implement some of these ideas if communities feel their state governments are not doing enough to safeguard local health.

An Overview of State Laws

Certain federal agencies and interested groups have examined information on state AFO regulations to justify their advocacy of additional federal regulations.[2] The results underscore the problems created by AFOs and suggest potential solutions to some of them. The evaluations generally center on water-quality issues and states' implementation of National Pollutant Discharge Elimination System programs.

Forty-five states have entered agreements with the EPA to administer a state NPDES or comparable program applicable to CAFOs. In the states not so authorized—Alaska, Idaho, Massachusetts, New Mexico, and Oklahoma—the EPA regional office implements and administers the NPDES program, but even these states may adopt regulations for CAFOs. Idaho, New Mexico, and Oklahoma have imposed state CAFOs requirements distinct from the federal NPDES requirements.

Twenty-five states authorized to administer an NPDES program have incorporated some other state permit, license, or authorization program.[3] The most common addition is a construction or operating permit. Some states have regional provisions where high concentrations of animals create a need for special regulations to preserve environmental quality. Other states rely on their own individualized non-NPDES programs. Only eleven states regulate CAFOs solely under a federal or state NPDES program: Alaska, Hawaii, Maine, Massachusetts, New Hampshire, New Jersey, Nevada, New York, Rhode Island, Tennessee, and West Virginia.

Five states—Indiana, Iowa, Kansas, Maryland, and North Carolina—have developed individual definitions of CAFOs for purposes of state regulations.[4] Iowa employs a classification scheme that considers the weight of animals and type of waste-control facility. Maryland incorporates an income requirement. Other states have lowered the number of animals triggering permit requirements.

Some common themes appear in all these state-level measures. Obviously nutrient and manure management is a major topic. Most states have regulations governing waste applied by irrigation, licensing and certification, lagoon design and maintenance, guarantees for closure of facilities, and odor controls. State regulations are especially significant when they go beyond federal requirements (see appendix 2 for a list of state CAFO regulations).

Nutrient and Manure Management

Significantly, state AFO provisions encourage using manure as a production resource rather than treating it as a waste by-product. Animal manure is an excellent source of nutrients for crops and enriches soil by supplying organic matter, augmenting water-holding capacity, and increasing fertility.[5] Progressive legislation recognizes that the application of manure to land is an established and recommended practice and implements criteria to advance sustainability, thus further encouraging producers to use nutrients from manure as production inputs. With this in mind, our federal government has adopted regulations that mandate comprehensive nutrient-management plans for CAFOs and has published recommendations for other AFOs. Some states have imposed mandatory manure-management requirements on additional operators.

Objectives

Nutrient- and manure-management programs have three major objectives: to help protect water quality, to reduce conflicts between agricultural producers and others, and to enhance crop performance. In the aggregate, most governmental regulations address the first two objectives, even though they provide operators some discretion in developing practices and implementing technology to reduce nutrient contamination. Although agriculture has traditionally used manure to enhance crop performance, excessive quantities of animal waste from CAFOs may require governments to take further action to advance the more provident use of this by-product.

Nutrient- and manure-management programs require consideration of waste, soils, and crops. Because repeated applications of manure can cause a nutrient to build up excessively, farmers need to calculate the nutrients in both the manure and the soil. They must also figure the amounts required for optimal crop production. This information lets farmers determine the amounts of manure to apply to individual fields. Applications of each major nutrient—nitrogen, phosphorus, and potassium—should be limited to recommended rates, for excessive nutrients can contribute to unnecessary water contamination. State Cooperative Extension Services and private firms provide user-friendly printouts of nutrient needs calculated from soil tests.

All this usually means that a farmer should apply only the quantity of manure required to reach the recommended amount of phosphorus, using an appropriate commercial fertilizer to alleviate deficiencies in the other nutrients. Using manure to meet all the nutrient needs of a crop will likely deposit excessive amounts of phosphorus, which can create environmental problems.

Additional Features

Maryland has supplemented its nutrient-management provisions with a poultry-litter matching service that attempts to reduce excessive amounts of phosphorus in four counties.[6] The state and commercial poultry producers are experimentally facilitating the transportation of poultry litter from farms that experience phosphorus overenrichment. In other areas, including north Georgia, an industry matching service helps find persons willing to receive poultry litter. The Georgia Poultry Federation has found a demand for poultry litter and has been able to match all excess litter with suitable outlets. These voluntary programs allow the transfer of excess phosphorus to fields where it will not create a pollution problem.

State nutrient- and manure-management provisions can go further and incorporate provisions prohibiting certain waste-disposal practices. For example, Illinois prohibits the application of manure within a quarter-mile of a home unless injected or incorporated in the ground on the day of application.[7] Moreover, manure cannot be applied within 200 feet of downslope surface water, within 150 feet of potable water-supply wells, and in certain other areas. Furthermore, Illinois precludes manure application in buffer zones related to surface waters and in every ten-year floodplain and limits the application of manure on snow-covered ground. North Carolina has embarked on a program to purchase conservation easements to remove swine operations from 100–year floodplains.[8]

Manure management, although bothersome and costly, is indispensable to the management of nutrients from animal waste. States have helped farmers by disseminating information on nutrient-management plans and by providing testing services. Specialists at soil and water conservation districts, the USDA's Natural Resources Conservation Service, and state Cooperative Extension Services all may help in developing manure-management plans.

Yet these efforts seem to have been insufficient. If we want to see more widespread use of practices that foster sustainable agriculture, we need to provide more encouragement. As it is, excessive amounts of phosphorus on some fields receiving manure bear witness to a breakdown in environmental stewardship practices. Rather than engaging in sustainable practices, farmers are disposing manure as a waste product. Short-term profitability objectives are both interfering with long-term productivity and degrading the environment. We need more definitive regulations.

Irrigation Systems and Agronomic-Rate Rules

Nutrient contamination problems from the application of liquid manure through irrigation systems are propelling states to regulate this activity. Manure placed on fields or applied as spray irrigation can percolate through soils to contaminate underlying aquifers. A survey of hog farmers in North Carolina revealed that only 40 percent had tested the content of their waste before applying it to the land.[9] An investigation of 1,595 drinking-water wells on property next to hog- and poultry-production facilities showed 10.2 percent of them to have nitrate levels above the current drinking-water standard of ten parts per million. If producers cannot or will not address such problems, governments must step in.

And indeed, some have. Iowa now regulates irrigation with liquid manure,[10] banning the practice except in certain limited situations. For example, manure may not be applied by spray irrigation on land located within an agricultural drainage-well area. Separation distances of 100 to 750 feet from specified land uses (such as residence) are required for the application of irrigated liquid manure.

Thirty-four states have enacted regulations requiring that CAFO waste be applied to land at agronomic rates.[11] By thus limiting the application of waste to the amount needed to meet a given crop's nitrogen or phosphorus requirements, these regulations help prevent the overuse of nutrients. To comply with the agronomic requirements, farmers must obtain data on the nutrients available in the manure, the soil, and the needs of the crop.

The state regulations on agronomic rates sound good, but in most cases they are incomplete. First, some cover only nitrogen, which leaves the overapplication of phosphorus as a potential problem. Second, many regulations apply only to CAFOs. Non-CAFOs, which include most animal-production facilities, are not regulated by the agronomic-rate rules. Third, the provisions face difficulties in implementation and enforcement. The lack of specific requirements means that few regulating authorities will be able to prove violations. In situations where excessive applications of animal waste are occurring, neighbors may push for more definitive controls, including regulations at the county or local level.

Licensing and Certification

State AFO legislation and regulations contain various requirements concerning the licensing and certification of persons operating livestock facilities or preparing nutrient-management plans. In general, state licensing requirements apply only to AFOs with more than some specified number of animals of a given species—often the same number the federal government uses to designate CAFOs.

Licensing provisions in Oklahoma exemplify a typical state or local licensing program. Operators whom the law covers are required to submit an animal-waste-management plan, an odor-abatement plan, a pest-management plan, a carcass-disposal plan, and an erosion-control plan.[12] To further protect neighbors, applicants must announce their license application to all property owners within one mile of the perimeter of a small AFO or two miles of a larger AFO. They must also submit a statement declaring their financial ability to operate, thus ensuring the availability of funds for remediation if environmental damages arise from their facility's activities.

Other states have attempted to reduce potential contamination problems through certification for persons operating AFOs. For example, North Carolina requires anyone running an AFO with more than 250 swine or 100 cattle to be certified to operate an animal-waste system.[13] Iowa requires the certification of commercial manure applicators and confinement-site manure applicators.[14] Illinois has established a certified livestock manager program to enhance management skills dealing with environmental awareness, safety, odor-control techniques and technology, best management practices, and manure-management plans.[15] All these provisions illustrate additional regulatory approaches that reduce pollution from AFOs.

Another approach involves education. Georgia requires training in best management practices, comprehensive nutrient-management planning, regulations and water-quality laws, standards and practices, siting, pollution prevention, monitoring, and record keeping.[16] The certification training may be performed by the state or another group. More than 95 percent of Georgia's poultry farmers have been certified in its Poultry Nutrient Management course.[17]

Perhaps the most rigorous requirements have been enacted by Maryland, whose Water Quality Improvement Act of 1998 mandates nutrient-management plans for agricultural operations with more than $2,500 in gross income and at least eight cows or comparable numbers of other animals.[18] Only persons whom the state's agriculture department licenses can prepare such plans. Moreover, contractors applying nutrients to agricultural land must be certified or perform work under a certified nutrient-management consultant. Applicators servicing more than ten acres of agricultural land that they own or manage must complete a state-run education program in nutrient application once every three years. Maryland's system thus includes the licensing of persons preparing the nutrient-management plans, the certification of nutrient applicators, and the registry of persons completing a nutrient-educational program.

Lagoons and Storage Structures

Everyone has heard horror stories of hog lagoons.[19] A lagoon in North Carolina spilled 25 million gallons of waste that killed up to 10 million fish and closed 364,000 acres of coastal wetlands to shellfishing.[20] North Carolina is still attempting to come to grips with the problems posed by animal-waste lagoons, and other states are even less prepared for lagoon catastrophes. Settlements with Smithfield Foods, Inc., and its North Carolina–based production companies (Murphy Farms, Inc.; Brown's of Carolina, Inc.; and Carrolls's Foods, Inc.) have resulted in the commitment of $15 million to the development of environmentally superior technologies for the management of swine waste.[21]

Lagoons provide a cost-effective manner to handle large quantities of animal waste. Large dairy and swine CAFOs deposit liquid animal waste in such lagoons, which hold the liquids until an appropriate time for applying them to fields. In some cases, they are pumped through an irrigation system onto pastures or croplands. In others, they are transferred to specialized equipment and deposited on fields.

Despite their advantages, lagoons can degrade the environment in three ways. First, they may allow waste to seep into groundwater, depositing excess nutrients in soil or water. Second, contamination by nutrients, sediments, or pathogens can result if improper operations or accidents allow lagoon contents to spill or be washed into surface waters. For example, an improperly maintained earthen dam may erode, allowing overflow; excessive rain from a hurricane may result in overflow as well. Third, as with solid waste, the improper application of liquid waste to land can contaminate ground- or surface waters.

Recent mishaps involving waste lagoons have spurred greater regulations, yet regulations in many states are too weak to preclude future environment disasters. Despite the environmental problems associated with lagoons, however, we cannot summarily abandon them. Lagoons constitute an important device for handling animal waste, especially for containing it when it should not be applied to land. Rather than proscribe lagoons, we should specify engineering standards for their design and prescribe other regulations to control potential contamination problems. Indeed, safeguards and siting restrictions for animal-waste lagoons should be similar to those in place for analogous industrial facilities, businesses, and sewage-treatment facilities.

Design Standards and Safeguards

Environmental concerns about waste lagoons and other manure-storage structures have led most states to adopt or at least consider regulations incorporating odor, design, and inspection safeguards. The most common safeguards comprise professional requirements for persons designing, operating, and inspecting manure-storage structures and lagoons. Generally this involves a qualified engineer.[22]

Scientific advances have altered the design and scale of lagoons considerably over the past twenty years. Lagoons have become larger, corresponding to increases in the numbers of animals at production facilities, and have incorporated new design specifications that make them less likely to fail. As a result, although the former development increases the risk of contamination, the latter greatly decreases it. Exceptions exist, however, in those states that have not adopted lagoon specifications.

The potential environmental contamination problems have prompted regulators to restrict the location of lagoons, prohibiting them, for example, in floodplains; Georgia, for instance, bans lagoons in 100–year floodplains. Still, these safeguards cannot prevent environmental problems following natural disasters, as when lagoons fail in times of extraordinary rainfall.

Some states are taking more drastic actions, moving toward prohibition. North Carolina has reached an agreement with its two largest pork producers to develop a replacement for lagoons and irrigated spray fields.[23] The state plans to eliminate the use of open-air lagoons entirely. A second idea, incorporated in a Georgia rule for swine operations with more than 7,500 swine (weighing over fifty-five pounds each), is to prohibit new swine CAFOs from having an uncovered lagoon.[24]

Inspections

In addition, states have responded by requiring lagoon inspections during both construction and operation. Typical provisions for new lagoons require inspection at least once during a preconstruction, construction, or postconstruction phase.

A more weighty question involves the inspection of existing lagoons. Inferior design standards and opportunities for maintenance lapses mean that we need to inspect older lagoons. Most animal-waste lagoons that fail and cause significant environmental damages were constructed prior to the design standards in use today. State monitoring programs, including inspections, provide the most practical way to address the potential short-comings of these older lagoons.

Some states' AFO provisions require annual or periodic inspections. Florida requires annual inspections; Arkansas, biennial ones.[25] But states often lack funds and staff to perform such a task. As with other ideas for improving our environment, the lack of funds limits what can be done. In many instances, therefore, officials inspect lagoons only if someone has complained. This mode of administration is unlikely to alleviate the environmental problems posed by older lagoons. States need to consider additional funding, including user fees, for inspections of lagoons so that they can fulfill their responsibility to protect public health.

Guarantees for Closure

Facilities for manure storage, including waste lagoons, are visible structures with a potential to contribute to environmental degradation. As with other, nonagricultural operations, this potential can increase when a facility shuts down, and news reports have led the public to view residual manure and nutrients at abandoned facilities as a likely source of environmental damage. In addition, experiences with other environmental problems have led states to impose provisions on guarantees and contingency funds to respond to possible environmental problems associated with discontinued operations.

Governments have enacted three types of regulatory provisions to address problems stemming from discontinued animal-production operations: financial responsibility, reserve funds, and combinations of these two. The intent behind these provisions is to ensure the proper disposal of manure and accompanying nutrients when storage facilities are closed. Some of these guarantees apply only to animal-waste lagoons. Other provisions, such as those in Indiana and Iowa, provide for the closure of all manure-storage structures.[26]

The financial-responsibility provisions include various avenues of accountability. Illinois allows operators to meet their responsibilities using a variety of instruments, including commercial or private insurance, guarantees, surety bonds, letters of credit, certificates of deposit, and designated savings accounts.[27] Georgia requires operators to provide detailed written estimates of closure costs and then establish a closure fund that can meet the estimated obligations.[28] By having operators place money in one or more of these instruments, the state ensures that funds will be available to remedy any environmental problems an operation may create, even if it is experiencing financial problems.

Taking a different approach, some states have established funds that can help pay to clean up qualifying sites. AFO owners and operators contribute to the fund in such an approach, and the state then draws from the fund when a property threatens the groundwater or other part of the environment. To reward conscientious management, the state may also return contributions to an owner or operator who successfully closes an operation.

Odor Controls and Setback Buffers

Odors from AFOs are a major issue that state legislatures are addressing through specific laws and administrative regulations. Air-quality degradation from swine operations is well documented. Poultry operations pose similar problems by releasing ammonia fumes. The issue is not merely aesthetic, however; some reports link odors and toxins emitted by AFOs to diarrhea, nausea, headaches, vomiting, teary eyes, and stuffy noses.[29] In addition, odors from swine farms have been found to adversely affect the moods of humans,[30] leading to anger, frustration, and otherwise poor psychological health.

Moderating Odors through Practices

Offensive odors may be addressed in three ways: (1) by preventing their creation, (2) by capturing or destroying them, and (3) by dispersing or disguising them.[31] Operators of AFOs have adopted numerous strategies to control odors. Some of the available strategies draw on relatively inexpensive technologies. Other technologies must await further development before they are cheap enough to use.

Manure produces more than eighty odorous compounds (gases) as it decomposes. People can detect low concentrations of some of these gasses, such as hydrogen sulfide (a rotten-egg smell). Others become noticeable only at high concentrations. Moreover, some combinations of gases are more foul than the sum of the constituents. Humans principally detect ammonia and sulfur compounds generated by microbial decomposition. Of course, these compounds occur in nature as well, but usually not in so great a quantity.

We know that odors vary with location, production practices, season, temperature, humidity, time of day, and wind conditions. This knowledge, together with information about odors from buildings and animal-holding facilities, manure storage and treatment, and manure applications, lets us devise strategies to moderate their intensity. Ventilation and proper cleaning can reduce odors for buildings and holding facilities. Covering manure pits with water can also reduce their emissions of ammonia and hydrogen sulfide. And we can reduce odors from lagoons by correctly correlating their size with the number of animals or by covering them.

When applying manure to fields, farmers can control the timing, location, and type of application, destroying odors before they reach humans. They should not apply manure on calm, humid days, when the odors will not dissipate. Using a rather obvious strategy, farmers can avoid applications when winds will carry the odors to neighbors, especially on weekends and holidays, when people want to enjoy their yards and engage in outdoor activities. In addition, injecting liquid manure into the soil reduces offensive odors, as does applying manure before plowing or cultivation, which inverts the waste under a layer of soil.

Legislating Odor Reduction

Legislatures and regulators have mandated certain practices in an attempt to reduce odors. Some provisions require AFOs to develop odor-abatement plans. Taking another tack, some states require the use of specific odor-control methods in given situations. For example, an Illinois law addresses odors accompanying manure removal, field application, lagoon construction, and holding structures.[32] Following yet another course, a North Carolina law allows the state to draft permanent odor-control rules based on required management practices and best management practices.[33]

Above all, however, legislative bodies have sought to reduce offensive odors via setback rules for AFOs. Regulators determine distances that new AFO facilities must maintain between their operations and various land uses. Distances required for setbacks are highly variable and, in a few cases, measured in miles. Unfortunately, there is little scientific justification for the specific distances stipulated. Nonetheless, public support for such measures have made them a prevalent response to AFO odor problems.

A more progressive idea involves using parametric formulas or dispersion models to calculate needed restrictions. Parametric formulas are based on parameters such as numbers of animals, housing systems, and the physical size of the operation.[34] Dispersion models can use inputs based on airborne emissions, weather conditions, and topography to establish setback distances. Formulas or models can achieve odor-control objectives without requiring all operators to institute the same setbacks, which can be excessive in some cases.

Beyond Animal-Waste Regulations

States have adopted numerous strategies in their efforts to control nutrient pollution from AFOs. While the state-by-state approach is cumber-
some and potentially inequitable, it allows for experimentation. Workable features of a program adopted by one state can serve as prototypes for
adoption in others.

A majority of state regulations adopt a "one-size-fits-all" approach.
They differentiate AFOs by numbers of animals and require large operations to adopt specific technology, manure-management systems, and
other practices whether they are polluting or not. By omitting meaningful consideration of housing type, topography, and climatic conditions,
the regulations are not oriented to actual pollution problems. For one
thing, we might require AFOs to alter practices only where there is a pollution problem. Furthermore, the absence of corresponding requirements
for crop producers overapplying commercial fertilizers complicates their
regulatory objectives.

The existing command-and-control, licensing, and certification provisions of state animal-waste regulations are eliminating some problems.
Nevertheless, existing regulations are insufficient because they fail to
embrace sustainability concepts, do not address applications of fertilizers,
and disregard market incentives to account for environmental costs.
Governments can do more to reduce the excessive amounts of nitrogen
and phosphorus that are impairing our waters. Indeed, where such problems exist, we may need regulations that govern all synthetic fertilizers
and additional sources of nutrients.

NOTES

1. Terence J. Centner, *Legal Structures Governing Animal Waste Management,*
White Papers on Animal Agriculture and the Environment (Raleigh, N.C.: National
Center for Manure and Animal Waste Management, 2002), ch. 15.

2. Environmental Protection Agency, *State Compendium: Programs and Regulatory
Activities Related to Animal Feeding Operations* (Washington, D.C.: EPA, 2001).

3. Ibid., 5.

4. Ibid., 12.

5. A. A. Araji, Z. O. Abdo, and P. Joyce, "Efficient Use of Animal Manure on Cropland—Economic Analysis," *Bioresource Technology* 79 (2001): 179–91.

6. *Maryland Agriculture Code Annotated* §8-704.2, 1999.

7. *Illinois Compiled Statutes Annotated,* ch. 510, §77/20.

8. North Carolina Department of Environment and Natural Resources, *Purchase
of Conservation Easements to Remove Swine Operations from the 100 Year Floodplain*
(Raleigh: State of North Carolina, 2000).

9. Natural Resource Defense Council, "America's Animal Factories: How States Fail to Prevent Pollution from Livestock Waste," North Carolina report (available at <http://www.nrdc.org/nrdc/nrdcpro/fppubl.html>), 1999.

10. *Iowa Code* §455B.165.

11. EPA, *State Compendium*, 11.

12. *Oklahoma Administrative Code,* title 35, ch. 17.

13. *North Carolina General Statutes* §§90A-47.1, 90A-47.2, 143–215.10B.

14. *Iowa Code* §455B.203A.

15. *Illinois Compiled Statutes Annotated,* ch. 510, §77/30.

16. *Georgia Compilation Rules and Regulations,* rule 391-3-6-.20(13).

17. "Farmers Recycle Poultry Litter," *Gainesville (Ga.) Times,* Sept. 26, 2002.

18. *1998 Maryland Laws,* chs. 324 and 325.

19. Robbin Marks, *Cesspools of Shame: How Factory Farm Lagoons and Sprayfields Threaten Environmental and Public Health* (Washington, D.C.: Natural Resources Defense Council and Clean Water Network, 2001).

20. Natural Resources Defense Council and Clean Water Network, *America's Animal Factories: How States Fail to Prevent Pollution from Livestock Waste* (available at <http://www.nrdc.org/water/pollution/factor/aafinx.asp>) (1998).

21. Smithfield Foods, Inc., "Smithfield, North Carolina AG Sign Historic Water Quality Compact," company press release, Raleigh, N.C., July 25, 2000.

22. *Illinois Compiled Statutes Annotated,* ch. 510, §77/15.

23. Associated Press, "Nation's Second-Largest Pork Producer Reaches Agreement with N.C.," wire service story, Oct. 3, 2000.

24. *Georgia Compilation Rules and Regulations,* rule 391-3-6-.20(8)(o).

25. EPA, *State Compendium*, 39, 68.

26. *Iowa Administrative Code,* rule 567-65.20.

27. *Illinois Compiled Statutes Annotated,* ch. 510, §77/17.

28. *Georgia Compilation Rules and Regulations,* rule 391-3-6-.20(11).

29. Marks, *Cesspools of Shame,* 19.

30. R. E. Sheffield and R.W. Bottcher, *Understanding Livestock Odors* (Raleigh: North Carolina Cooperative Extension Service, AG-589, 1999).

31. Ibid.

32. *Illinois Compiled Statutes Annotated,* ch. 510, §77/25.

33. *North Carolina Administrative Code,* title 15, rules 2D.1801–2D.1804.

34. Larry D. Jacobson, S. L. Wood, D. R. Schmidt, A. J. Heber, J. R. Bicudo, and R. D. Moon, *Site Selection of Animal Operations Using Air Quality Criteria,* White Papers on Animal Agriculture and the Environment (Raleigh, N.C.: National Center for Manure and Animal Waste Management, 2002), ch. 2.

6 The Environment of Rural America

*W*e had an apple orchard for a few years of my youth. I remember picking a variety of apples and savoring their different tastes: Red Astrakhans for the first taste of fresh apples in midsummer, mellow Cortlands and crisp McIntoshes for the fall, staid Romes stored for the winter months, and tart Rhode Island Greenings for applesauce and pies. Each fall my parents would lug a few bushels of apples to the cellar to be used during the winter months. Winter breakfasts often included fresh applesauce.

But my family's favorite memories of apples come from our cider-making parties. Forty years later uncles and cousins still talk about them. My parents would schedule the party on a Sunday afternoon in October. A few days before the event we would gather windfalls and make sure they were clean. You need a lot of apples to make cider, so we would get permission from a neighbor to gather windfalls from his orchard. We would ride the trailer through the pasture and across Canadaway Creek and fill our bushels in the orchard. After using the grass to wipe off any dirt or *earthworms sticking to the apples, we would fill the bushel baskets, and Dad would set them on the trailer. Then we would ride home, trying not to lose any apples from the heaped containers as the trailer bounced through the creek and pasture.*

The next job was to get the cider press out of the barn. We would set it on the back lawn and wash it together with the apples. This could have been fun, but it was always too cold. Finally the big day would arrive. Uncles, aunts, cousins, and friends would arrive and help with the work. My brother and I would greet our cousins and look around for things to do. We were all younger than ten years old, so there was little we could do. Instead, we waited for some fun. The apple remains provided the medium.

The apples were crushed and then dumped into a slatted container for pressing into cider. After a batch of apples had been pressed, the crushed remains were deposited into a wheelbarrow and taken to a hill in an adjacent pasture. An uncle or someone else would dump them at the top of the hill and we would push them down with a shovel. We all watched the first adventurous cousin run down the hill through the apple remains. Then he would dare another cousin to do the same. The first run through one batch of apple remains was easy, and no one fell. But as remains were added to the pile, it became increasingly harder not to slip into the sticky mess. Everyone eventually fell and slid on the remains. What tacky clothes we presented to our moms after this entertainment.

As our childhood fun shows, small amounts of apple remains were manageable, but greater amounts yielded tumbling children and soiled clothes. In a similar manner, when farmers raise only a few animals, their manure does not overwhelm nature's ability to handle the nutrients. As more animals are added in one location, however, their manure may overwhelm fields and streams, leading to nutrient pollution.

The adults in the family saw us playing in the remains, but they never stopped us. Our mothers simply cleaned up both the children and the clothes. Correspondingly, farmers often realize that their activities have a potential to degrade the environment. They decline to alter their practices, however, out of economic self-interest (and sometimes to ensure their very survival). It's usually the general public who must respond to the pollutants and damaged resources.

Agriculture as a Polluter

The by-products that accompany the production of our country's plentiful foodstuffs make polluters of our farms. Today agriculture is the single
largest source of water impairment from human activities.[1] This was not
the case back in the 1960s, when our worst pollution came from wastes
produced by factories and cities. In 1972 Congress passed the Clean Water Act to protect our water resources from environmental degradation.
This act has evolved into a complex set of regulations to reduce point-
source pollution. Command-and-control mechanisms preclude the disposal of contaminants. Technology-based effluent limitations serving as
performance standards may be required to reduce pollutants leaving a site.

These regulations eliminated much of the existing point-source pollution in the United States, leaving non-point-source pollution as the
major cause of river and lake pollution. Non-point-source pollution,
which is diffuse, derives from several sectors, including agriculture, for-
estry, urban development, mining, and construction activities. All these
sectors pollute our waters, but agriculture certainly does its share: the leading pollutants of rivers and streams are siltation, pathogens, and nutrients.[2] More than 69 percent of America's impaired river miles contain
pollutants from agriculture.[3] Except for the Great Lakes, moreover, 50
percent of impaired lake acres contain pollution from agricultural activities.[4] (Impaired waters are those not fully supporting their EPA designated
uses, such as swimming or drinking.)

Of course, simply producing a pollutant need not constitute a problem. Indeed, we routinely permit some discharges of contaminants—otherwise we couldn't drive our cars. In any event, all activities and biotic
systems—including natural ecosystems—cause pollution, and agricultural production is no exception. The question should be not whether
something produces pollutants but rather what we can and should do to
ameliorate or terminate the adverse effects of egregious contamination.

At the same time, data suggest that agriculture might appropriately be
subjected to more regulations to control pollutant discharges, for although
our large-scale agricultural-production and food policies provide us with
cheap food products, they do so at significant environmental costs. Because agricultural production employs large land areas, it produces pollutants from a variety of visible activities, including tillage; applications of fertilizers, manure, and pesticides; irrigation; and use of feedlots. For example,
the use of synthetic fertilizers has been accompanied by a reduction of the
water-holding capacity of soils and increases in soil nutrient loss.[5]

Other major issues include the overuse of pesticides and the loss of biodiversity. Moreover, concerns about recombinant bovine somatotropin and genetically engineered organisms have led to public outcry against the use and application of these products. Some citizens would like to forgo technology they see as posing potential environmental problems. Public responses to these technological advances may presage legislative reactions, including more stringent regulations of undesirable features.

Water Contamination

The major environmental problem accompanying animal production involves water contamination by nitrogen and phosphorus. The specialized production of animals at AFOs generates excess manure, which has become a problem. Manure is especially rich in these nutrients, so that careless practices can create pollution. Nitrates are water soluble, allowing them to leach into groundwater or run off into surface water. Phosphorus is less mobile, but excessive soil concentrations can still pose problems. In fact, research has shown that overapplying manure on cropland increases the amounts of nitrogen and phosphorus in ground- and surface waters, and these excess nutrient levels (eutrophication) can lead to increased algae growth that depletes water's dissolved oxygen (hypoxia). Algae, whether living or dead, can block sunlight required by other vegetative species, killing both vegetation and fish.

First, consider nitrogen, high levels of which often appear in the soil. In fact, levels in some areas of the United States are so high that costly purification systems are being installed to protect humans.[6] In many areas of northern Europe, moreover, the soil contains so much nitrogen that plants cannot take up additional amounts.[7] The reason for these high nitrogen concentrations is overapplication. Plants—including food crops—need this nutrient for optimal growth. To ensure that plants have sufficient quantities of nitrogen, people (including home gardeners and suburbanites desiring green lawns) overapply it. With a well-defined industry providing fertilizer products at low prices, it is cheaper to overapply fertilizer than to suffer reduced yields due to insufficient nutrients.

This nitrogen then ends up in bodies of water, indirectly causing fish kills, reducing marine diversity, and contributing to global warming. The results can be substantial. For example, the nutrient-laden waters of the Mississippi River basin cause the Gulf of Mexico to undergo seasonal hypoxia in an area the size of New Jersey.[8] This oxygen depletion, which renders the area uninhabitable for many aquatic species and threatens commercial and recreational fishing, stems at least in part from the river's increasing annual nitrate amounts, which have tripled since 1950.[9] Studies have found that agricultural activities are the largest contributors of this increase in nitrogen, with approximately 15 percent of the nitrogen flux coming from animal operations.[10]

Second, consider phosphorus, which also contributes to eutrophication. Since it is cheaper to prevent eutrophication than to remedy its effects, governments are seeking to reduce phosphorus entering water bodies, including phosphorus from AFOs. Nevertheless, although soil testing and a phosphorus index provide information on quantities of phosphorus, correlations to water pollution are nebulous. Phosphorus loss is a hydrological problem, for different soils and sites transfer phosphorus into waters at different rates. It is thus more important to control runoff and soil erosion through management practices than to manipulate production practices to achieve desired soil-test results.

Nutrient Problems Connected to AFOs

AFOs have problems with nitrogen and phosphorus because they concentrate animals at individual facilities and regions. Because manure is bulky, its use as fertilizer is economically feasible only if it is applied near its production. CAFOs, however, produce too much manure for surrounding fields. Some producers use neighbors' cropland, but others do not have a good option for disposing of manure. Manure and liquids from feedlots can thus become a waste by-product that, when overapplied to fields, discharges nutrients into the environment. Although a watershed might be able to handle the nutrients from one or two CAFOs, several CAFOs in close proximity can overwhelm the watershed's capacity.

Researchers have analyzed the locations of CAFOs in our country, finding that some areas have surplus nutrients with a potential to cause water contamination.[11] First, they calculated the nitrogen and phosphorus produced by animals at existing CAFOs for each county. They then determined available crop acreage in each county. Assuming that the manure from the animal operations was spread on lands within the same county, the data indicate that 35 counties have too much nitrogen and 107 counties have too much phosphorus for available crop acreage.

Furthermore, some AFO operators are spreading manure on fields in the fall or winter, when it cannot be used by crops.[12] For cornfields receiving manure applications in the winter, up to 15 percent of the phosphorus may be lost.[13] Finally, problems may emerge in other ways as well. Liquid-manure-handling systems beget problems of seepage, accidental overflows, odor emissions, pathogen releases, embankment failures, and abandonment of lagoons.

Our federal and state governments have been hesitant to micro-manage manure disposal, but some European governments have been more enterprising. Since 1986 the Netherlands has sought to limit nitrogen loss from agricultural land by restricting the amount of manure allowed per acre.[14] Other European governments have restricted the number of animals per acre of cultivated land.[15] More recently the Netherlands banned manure spreading in winter months and required covers over manure-storage facilities.[16]

European researchers have also devised methods to reduce nutrient outputs per animal. Research on phosphorus digestibility has allowed Dutch producers to halve the excretion of phosphorus per growing pig.[17] Ammonia emissions from poultry have been reduced through the introduction of low-emission housing and manure-application techniques.[18]

Animals in Water Bodies

Farmers and ranchers who allow their livestock to graze in streams and riparian areas can also threaten water quality. First, the livestock foul waters with their waste. Obviously, we don't want urine or manure deposited directly into surface waters being used for drinking or recreational purposes. The public and regulators have thus proposed and adopted regulations to exclude livestock from these bodies of water. Some of these regulations include riparian zones adjacent to public water supplies.

Second, livestock with access to streams and riparian areas can destroy vegetation that helps maintain water quality. Their hooves trample and kill vegetation as they enter and exit surface waters, and vegetation not killed outright is left so damaged that it cannot provide food and cover for wildlife. In addition, stream banks denuded of vegetation, especially mature plants, are more prone to erosion. This degrades the water by filling it with sediments. Animals entering and exiting the water exacerbate this problem, for their hooves churn up the soil at the bottom of the stream, releasing sediments to muddy the water.

Third, livestock can adversely affect water temperature. By preventing shrubs and trees from reaching maturity, livestock eliminate sources of shade. This can markedly raise the temperature of streams or small bodies of water to the detriment of cold-water fish species. Banning livestock from defined riparian zones can thus protect native plant and fish species as well as water quality.

In a lawsuit that highlighted public interest in keeping animals from streams,[19] environmental organizations in Oregon challenged the federal government's failure to prevent livestock from grazing along certain public areas of rivers protected under the Wild and Scenic Rivers Act. The environmentalists showed that the health of cold-water fish was linked to the vitality of water and vegetation, which had been impaired because of denuded and collapsed streambanks caused by livestock. They also demonstrated that grazing had damaged native plants and plant communities. Because the Bureau of Land Management had failed to adopt a river plan that balanced continued grazing with protecting and enhancing river values, the court ruled the federal government to be violating the Wild and Scenic Rivers Act.

Another demonstration of the public's interest in this matter was the Clean Streams Initiative, a 1996 ballot initiative considered by the voters of Oregon.[20] The initiative sought to prohibit livestock in state waters and designated riparian zones if the animals would contribute to the violation of water-quality standards and the waterway had been identified as "water-quality limited." Riparian zones of up to one hundred feet on either side of the stream could have been designated. Ultimately, however, the initiative was defeated.

Nevertheless, the initiative's ideas remain as possibilities for future conservation proposals. Although unsuccessful, the initiative advanced new options for improving the environment for native fish populations. Governments can establish riparian buffers barring animals from grazing next to some streams. Such buffers can safeguard our natural resources and prevent pollution.

Of course, just because producers may graze animals in vulnerable areas does not mean they will. Many farmers have voluntarily fenced off riparian buffers. Especially in the upper Midwest and the East, the curtailment of livestock from streams has markedly improved water quality in countless watersheds. Moreover, CAFOs themselves tend to remove large numbers of livestock from streams and riparian zones.

Yet the unresolved issue is financial: who should pay for riparian buffers where they do not already exist? Buffers cost money and restrict the use of land. Custom has recognized landowners' rights to graze their animals freely in riparian areas. If this right is terminated by the government, should landowners be compensated? Given the economic burdens of buffers, we may expect the conflicts between grazing and environmental quality to continue.

In fact, keeping animals out of streams may not be the best solution. Research shows that streams in some forested landscapes have more erosion than streams with grassy banks.[21] This suggests that it might be better to let animals graze next to streams and thus maintain grass along the banks. Still, favorable results would require controlled grazing, with the livestock allowed to forage next to the stream only at carefully selected times.[22] Such findings show the difficulties in prescribing agronomic practices. Agriculture is a management- and information-intensive enterprise.[23] Rather than prescribe practices, we should perhaps work with farmers in developing their capacity to adopt practices suitable for their farms.

Best Management Practices

Farmers, researchers, and governments have pursued numerous methods to minimize agricultural degradation of water quality. One response involves using best management practices (BMPs). Conservation and other practices can reduce water and air pollution from agricultural and other land-disturbing activities. Cooperative Extension Service specialists help farmers learn about and implement BMPs to reduce agricultural contamination, and Congress and state legislatures have instituted several different conservation programs to provide incentive for adopting BMPs.

Although variously defined, BMPs generally comprise those practices determined to be the most effective practical means for preventing pollution or reducing pollutants to levels compatible with water-quality goals. Federal law defines BMPs as "schedules of activities, prohibitions of practices, maintenance procedures, and other management practices to prevent or reduce the pollution of 'waters of the United States.' BMPs also include treatment requirements, operating procedures, and practices to control plant site runoff, spillage or leaks, sludge or waste disposal, or drainage from raw material storage."[24] Most BMPs minimize water pollution through the application of ecologically sound conservation principles. They do not, however, supersede state water-quality standards.

Nevertheless, costs and other factors mean that producers fail to use BMPs on millions of acres of farmland. Landowners may see little or no direct benefit from adopting BMPs, even though they incur all the costs. This situation has led governments to adopt programs whereby landowners are paid to initiate BMPs.

More than forty BMPs have been widely associated with conservation and stewardship measures. Several are important in responding to water-quality problems associated with crop and animal production. The current unacceptable levels of pollution from agriculture and AFOs might prompt us to inquire whether further reliance on BMPs could help reduce environmental degradation.

Contour Farming and Terracing

Perhaps the most celebrated BMP is the erosion-control practice of contour farming, which involves orienting furrows across the slope on or near the level rather than up and down the slope. Anyone driving through agricultural areas set in a rolling landscape has viewed the results of this practice. Contour farming, which is most suitable on uniformly sloping fields, can markedly reduce runoff from land-applied manure. Terracing serves as a similar BMP. Terraces are earthen embankments constructed on the contour or across a slope to intercept runoff.

Since the 1930s our government has worked with farmers to encourage the use of contour farming and terracing where the terrain slopes. These practices have direct agronomic benefits, for they help retain a farm's fertility and value. As a result, farmers have adopted them widely in many areas. In addition, contour farming and terracing are critical for alleviating the runoff of nutrients that can accompany applications of manure from AFOs.

Filter Strips and Grassed Waterways

Farmers have also embraced the use of filter strips to preserve their soil resources. These strips of perennial vegetation are located downslope from cropland, so that they intercept flowing surface water or shallow groundwater. In doing so, filter strips improve water quality by cleansing the runoff of sediment, organic material, and other pollutants, including nutrients from animal waste.

Generally, the vegetative growth of a filter strip should be harvested and removed to encourage more growth and remove the nutrients and other contaminants that have accumulated in the plant tissue. Filter-strip areas in which considerable sediment deposition occurs will need to be periodically regraded to restore the slope necessary for the strip to function properly.

Another BMP, contour grass strips, borrows elements from contour farming and filter strips. This technique alternates narrow buffer strips of permanent herbaceous cover with broader cultivated strips that are farmed on the contour. These strips reduce sheet and rill erosion, slow runoff, and trap sediment, serving the environment in the same manner as do filter strips.

Grassy areas for drainage of surface waters constitute a slightly different technique. Grassed waterways are permanent drainage paths of perennial grasses designed to protect soil from erosion by concentrated water flows. They provide for the water disposal from terraces, diversions, or other concentrated flow areas. Such waterways are one of the most widely used conservation buffer types, with approximately 1.6 million acres devoted to this practice.[25] Besides controlling erosion, grassed waterways provide benefits similar to those enumerated for filter strips.

Conservation Tillage

Conservation tillage, an important agricultural practice for reducing soil erosion, is a cultivation method wherein at least 30 percent of the soil surface is covered with crop residues. Conservation tillage also conserves moisture. Unfortunately, since producers who employ it often increase their use of herbicides, this practice may increase pesticide transfer to groundwater.

Continued research on conservation tillage is providing additional information on the merits of this practice. The USDA had hoped that 50 percent of the land producing soybeans, corn, cotton, sorghum, wheat, rice and other annual crops might be planted using conservation tillage by the year 2002.[26] The results have fallen short of those hopes, however. In 1998 only 37 percent of the land for these crops was prepared under a conservation-tillage method.

Pasture Management

Most ranchers are aware of measures to improve the quality and quantity of forage in pastures. Pasture management generally involves selecting plant species, determining stocking rates, applying nutrients, and controlling weeds. Alternatively, management techniques can increase the quantity and quality of herbage for livestock. This often results in a more efficient conversion of feed into animal product. In some areas pasture management is beneficial in helping preserve native vegetation and habitats.

New research on range management and management techniques shows that ranchers may manage livestock and plant populations to maximize animal production. Grazing rotations and adjustments in stocking rates can increase overall productivity or improve livestock distribution. Although occasional heavy grazing may be economical, most farmers strive to avoid permanently damaging rangeland plant communities by heavy grazing. For some areas farmers may drill or cast seed to augment existing pastures.

Pasture management may also involve practices to control erosion and pollution caused by livestock. For example, fences can prevent meandering livestock from destroying vegetation near water sources, degrading water quality, or interfering with recreational activities. Fences also may be used to maintain riparian buffers, enhancing water quality by keeping manure, nutrients, and sediments from streams and other water bodies.

Riparian Buffers

Some of the environmental benefits of riparian buffers alongside bodies of water have already been enumerated. Such buffers, which consist of trees, woody shrubs, and other vegetation, ameliorate pollution by filtering and eliminating elements from water. Buffers remove sediment and suspended solids from surface-water runoff. Some vegetative species in a riparian buffer transform nitrate to nitrogen gas and reduce nitrogen in runoff by as much as 80 percent.[27] Plants may take up nutrients and sequester them in plant tissues. Riparian buffers can also help transform toxic chemicals into nontoxic forms via microbial decomposition, oxidation, reduction hydrolysis, solar radiation, and other biodegrading forces.

Riparian forest buffers generate shade, lowering water temperatures and thus improving habitat for fish and other aquatic species. Because these benefits aid many fish species, buffer recommendations exist for streams in national forests. Wetlands may also serve as a riparian buffer. Research on wetland buffers shows they can function well in removing sediments and nutrients from drainage water. A wetland simulation model concluded that wetlands can remove 79 percent of the nitrogen and phosphorus in drainage waters from an agricultural area.[28] Plants and animals then take up these nutrients.

Waste-Management Systems and Programs

The BMPs of waste-management systems dictate facilities and procedures used to store manure and other waste products for timely application to agricultural land. Liquid-manure lagoons and storage structures for slurry manure are major components of waste-management systems. These BMPs also govern facility design, procedures, and application of agricultural waste.

With waste-management systems in place, further planning is needed for the application of the waste. A comprehensive nutrient-management plan can coordinate the use of manure as a crop input rather than an unwanted by-product. Researchers may suggest that manure be spread once or twice a year, as needed by crops, making it more likely that the manure-borne nutrients will be used by growing crops.

Livestock facilities with organic waste such as dead poultry may need to adopt a composting process. This process can stabilize the organic matter, reduce odors, preserve nutrients, and prepare the matter for handling or spreading. Composting allows waste to be utilized on-farm as a nitrogen-bearing soil amendment, with land application to be conducted at an appropriate time.

Cover Crops

Another conservation practice that our government has advocated for generations is the use of cover crops. While farmers often know about cover crops, specialization, large-scale production, and short-term objectives have resulted in widespread disregard of this practice. Cover crops consist of grasses, legumes, or small grains that farmers plant to protect or improve the soil. The vegetative cover helps prevent soil erosion in the absence of the main crop, and afterward farmers can incorporate the residues into the soil.

Cover crops may be especially important after the harvest of a low-residue-producing crop, such as soybeans or corn cut for silage. They can provide seasonal protection for soils and forage for wildlife.

Crop Rotation

By planting a series of different crops on a particular field, farmers can augment soil quality and control some pests, diseases, and weeds without the use of pesticides. Rotation may improve soil quality by creating different types of residues. For example, a legume may enhance soil nitrogen for a subsequent crop. In addition, crop rotation can provide farmers with superior pest control, giving certain predators and parasites the ecological diversity they need. Rotations help control weeds by smothering them, and plant residues may also reduce weed concentrations. Finally, plant-plant and plant-microorganism interactions may be beneficial for subsequent crops. With specialized animal and crop production, monocultures have replaced crop rotations, with the corresponding loss of benefits from this husbandry practice.

Pesticides

The publication of *Silent Spring* brought the problem of pesticide contamination to light. Congress responded with new legislation authorizing detailed pesticide regulations. In a major blow to agriculture, the power to regulate pesticides was moved from the USDA to the EPA. Revisions to the Federal Insecticide, Fungicide, and Rodenticide Act made it more difficult to register new pesticide products and easier to cancel their registrations. Yet water contamination by pesticides remains a major public issue. Agricultural pesticides have been identified as pollutants of groundwater in thirty states.[29]

Some of this groundwater pollution stems from the application of pesticides in the production of agricultural crops. This type of contamination is characterized as non-point-source pollution. Although limited research directly links levels of pesticides and degree of groundwater contamination, the numerous locations with documented pesticide contamination of groundwater have prompted governmental researchers and private firms to continue seeking ways to reduce pesticide use. BMPs, such as filter strips and buffers, have been effective in removing some pesticides from surface and groundwater. Ongoing integrated pesticide-management efforts are curtailing the use of pesticides. Other scientific achievements are facilitating pest-eradication programs, such as the elimination of the boll weevil in some states, that can lessen the need for pesticides. These and other biotechnological engineering efforts are expected to reduce pesticide usage in the future. Simultaneously, specialized animal and crop production have increased the use of pesticides. Thus, efforts to move to diversified farming practices might reduce the need for pesticides.

Loss of Biodiversity

The loss of biodiversity due to the destruction of habitats, species extinction, and loss of genetic material constitutes yet another environmental concern. Without the species and genetic materials we are currently obliterating, future generations may have difficulty in sustaining life as we know it. More significantly, scientists have perfected "Terminator" gene technology.[30] Seed companies may modify seeds by adding a gene that prevents reseeding the plant. Growers will thus be unable to save seed for future crops. Instead, they will have to buy new seed from the company, a potentially catastrophic proposition for poor farmers in Third World countries. "Terminator" may become the new byword for failure among impoverished farmers.[31]

The genetic diversity of major food crops is an important issue for agriculture. The biotechnological revolution has embraced the breeding of plants and animals to increase food production. During the last century plant breeding and genetic engineering quadrupled yields of corn, sorghum, and potatoes.[32] Rice, soybeans, wheat, cotton, and sugarcane yields doubled. Nonetheless, agriculture's support for genetically modified crops may not be as propitious as the firms marketing these products claim. American farmers may inadvertently be establishing conditions that foster crop failure, detract from sustainability, shrivel genetic resources, and undermine farming methods in Third World countries.

In the rush to compete in the international marketplace, American producers are creating monocultures by selecting genetically engineered species. Monocultural crops are extremely vulnerable to diseases and pests. A new species of corn leaf blight in 1970 demonstrated the danger of such monocultures.[33] A single adversity, such as a new pathogen, can lead to a major crop disaster. Such a calamity may cause a major upheaval in our country's grain production and food markets.

Genetically engineered crops may present dangers beyond those concerning monocultured crops, affecting other species as well. Will genetically modified crops annihilate native species? Recently traces of DNA from genetically modified corn were reported in remote cornfields in Oaxaca, Mexico.[34] Although transgenic crops were not supposed to move from the fields where they were planted, samples from Mexico seem to contain a DNA segment from a bioengineered variety. This suggests that native species are threatened by genetically modified varieties. Genes from a genetically engineered crop may cross-pollinate with native crops and destroy species that are particularly well suited for the locale. Pollen from a genetically engineered crop could modify a weed species to create an insect-proof, hard-to-kill species.[35]

NOTES

1. Environmental Protection Agency, *The Quality of Our Nation's Water: 1996* (Washington, D.C.: EPA, 1999), 13.

2. Environmental Protection Agency, *National Water Quality Inventory: 1998 Report to Congress* (Washington, D.C.: EPA, 2000), 61.

3. U.S. Department of Agriculture, *Agriculture and Water Quality* (Washington, D.C.: USDA, 1999).

4. Ibid.

5. Nicholas R. Jordan, "Sustaining Production with Biodiversity," in *The Farm as a Natural Habitat: Reconnecting Food Systems with Ecosystems,* ed. Dana L. Jackson and Laura L. Jackson (Washington, D.C.: Island, 2002), 157.

6. United Nations Environment Programme, *Global Environment Outlook 2000* (see <http://unep.org/geo2000>) (2000).

7. Ibid.

8. Donald A. Goolsby and William A. Battaglin, *Nitrogen in the Mississippi Basin—Estimating Sources and Predicting Flux to the Gulf of Mexico,* Fact Sheet 135-00 (Washington, D.C.: U.S. Geological Survey, 2000).

9. Ibid.

10. Donald A. Goolsby et al., *Flux and Sources of Nutrients in the Mississippi-Atchafalaya River Basin,* Coastal Ocean Program Decision Analysis Series, no. 17 (Washington, D.C.: National Oceanic and Atmospheric Administration, 1999), xvi.

11. Charles H. Lander, David Moffitt, and Klaus Alt, *Nutrients Available from Livestock Manure Relative to Crop Growth Requirements,* Natural Resources Conservation Service (Washington, D.C.: USDA, 1998).

12. Tom Horton, "Farms, Water Quality Can Prosper Together," *Baltimore Sun,* Dec. 7, 2001, p. 2B.

13. Donald W. Meals, "Watershed-Scale Response to Agricultural Diffuse Pollution Control Programs in Vermont, USA," *Water Science and Technology* 33, no. 4 (1996): 197–204.

14. O. Oenema et al., "Leaching of Nitrate from Agriculture to Groundwater: The Effect of Policies and Measures in the Netherlands," *Environmental Pollution* 102 (1998): 471–78.

15. A. W. Jongbloed, N. P. Lenis, and Z. Mroz, "Impact of Nutrition on Reduction of Environmental Pollution by Pigs: An Overview of Recent Research," *Veterinary Quarterly* 19, no. 3 (1997): 130–34.

16. J. J. Neeteson, "Nitrogen and Phosphorus Management on Dutch Dairy Farms: Legislation and Strategies Employed to Meet the Regulations," *Biology and Fertility of Soils* 30 (2000): 566–72.

17. Jongbloed et al., "Impact of Nutrition," 130.

18. I. J. M. De Boer, P. L Van Der Togt, M. Grossman, and R. P. Kwakkel, "Nutrient Flows for Poultry Production in the Netherlands," *Poultry Science* 79 (2000): 172–79.

19. Oregon Natural Desert Association v. Bureau of Land Management, 953 F. Supp. 1133, 1145 (D. Ore. 1997).

20. Oregon Measure 38, Prohibits Livestock in Certain Polluted Waters or on Adjacent Lands, ballot initiative, State of Oregon, 1996.

21. Brian A. DeVore, "When Farmers Shut Off the Machinery," in *The Farm as a Natural Habitat,* ed. Jackson and Jackson, 94.

22. Ibid., 94.

23. George M. Boody, "Agriculture as a Public Good," in *The Farm as a Natural Habitat,* ed. Jackson and Jackson, 265.

24. *Code of Federal Regulations,* title 40, §122.2.

25. Herby Bloodworth and Jeri L. Berc, *Cropland Acreage, Soil Erosion, and Installation of Conservation Buffer Strips: Preliminary Estimates of the 1997 National Resources Inventory,* National Resources Inventory (Washington, D.C.: USDA, 1997).

26. Conservation Technology Information Center, *1998 Crop Residue Management Executive Summary* (West Lafayette, Ind.: CTIC, 1998).

27. Lewis L. Osborne and David A. Kovacic, "Riparian Vegetated Buffer Strips in Water-Quality Restoration and Stream Management," *Freshwater Biology* 29 (1993): 243–47.

28. G. M. Cheschir, R. W. Skaggs, and J. W. Gilliam, "Evaluation of Wetland Buffer Areas for Treatment of Pumped Agricultural Drainage Water," *Transactions of the American Society of Agricultural Engineers* 35 (1992): 175–82.

29. Sandra Batie, W. E. Cox, and P. L. Diebel, *Managing Agricultural Contamination of Groundwater: State Strategies* (Washington, D.C.: National Governors' Association, 1989).

30. Jeffrey Kluger, "The Suicide Seeds," *Time,* Feb. 1, 1999, pp. 44–45.

31. "Terminator Genes: Fertility Rights," *The Economist,* Oct. 9, 1999, p. 104.

32. World Resources Institute, "Agriculture and Genetic Diversity" (available at <http://www.wri.org/biodiv/agrigene.html>), Oct. 18, 2001.

33. Clifton E. Anderson, "Genetic Engineering: Dangers and Opportunities," *The Futurist,* Mar.–Apr. 2000, pp. 20–25.

34. David Quist and Ignacio H. Chapela, "Transgenic DNA Introgressed into Traditional Maize Landraces in Oaxaca, Mexico," *Nature* 414 (Nov. 29, 2001): 541.

35. Anderson, "Genetic Engineering," 20.

7   Agricultural Conservation Efforts

*W*oods ought to be peaceful and quiet: ours aren't. They're bounded on the south by Interstate 90. The noise of its traffic overpowers the serenity of the wooded creek setting. Although we have planted trees as screens, they cannot suppress the commotion from the trucks and other vehicles. Fortunately, the traffic does not mask the woodsy smells or sights. And the noise does not detract from the opportunities for working with nature to create a more beautiful setting. Our woods have given us endless hours of pleasure. Until recently, they were used almost daily for nature walks, during which we could see deer and birds, including wild turkeys.

Our woods contain more than just trees. One part is replete with trees, but another part is swampy, and yet another part consists of a field abandoned during the early part of the last century. In some areas we battle the wild grape vines that continuously attempt to smother the trees. In a few areas we seek to preserve a particular setting that is conducive to the ground pine covering the forest floor.

In other areas we preserve wildflowers. Bouquets of adder's tongue and spring beauty provide a fragrant springtime setting.

Parts of the abandoned field were used for new plantings. Scots and jack pine were selected to screen off the interstate—these trees grow quickly and add a rich pine aroma to the air. We planted red spruce and douglas firs to provide boughs for the Christmas season. We added white pines, with their lovely soft needles, and larches, with their delicate green spring growth and golden yellow fall color. And we added oaks, catalpa, and other trees for variety.

Other parts of the abandoned field were allowed to return to woodland, although not without some direction. We used a chainsaw to remove some of the poplars and willows in favor of maples and oaks. We thinned some of the trees that had double crowns or were too close together. We retained the wild apple, mountain ash, and hemlock for the wildlife. We saved maples for their potential value as hardwoods. With these efforts, we created a wide wooded buffer extending from the neighbor's cornfields to Beaver Creek.

No new plantings have occurred for several years. Mother Nature is in control and sends a continuous supply of new seedlings to compete with the established flora. Although a few of the mature tulip poplars, maples, and oaks were harvested to make room for numerous saplings reaching for more light, the forested habitat remained a feast for the senses. You can still enjoy a diversity of tree species, fruit-bearing shrubs, uncommon wildflowers, and other flora. We have a refuge for animals to seek cover from the surrounding fields and vineyards—and the interstate.

My family's wooded reserve reflected my parents' efforts to operate a business while preserving native resources and the beauty of the countryside. By retaining this natural area for recreational activities and enjoyment, my parents helped preserve habitats for native animals and plants. But the more important efforts involved the conservation of the farm's soil resources and practices affecting the two creeks that traversed parts of the farm. My parents sought to employ appropriate stewardship practices so that the farm would not lose any of its productive capacity. For the creeks, a major goal was to maintain their banks and prevent erosion that would carry topsoil downstream.

Specialization Challenges Conservation

Unfortunately, not all farmers have followed my family's example. Encouraged to plant fencerow to fencerow in the 1970s and now and then given guarantees for commodity prices, farmers have been led to adopt practices inimical to conservation. They have been encouraged to specialize in row crops, abandoning livestock production and plowing up pastures as a result. They have been encouraged to plant row crops on highly erodible lands, leading to erosion problems. Some have removed fencerows, shrubs and trees to amass their acreages into large fields. Landscapes of row crops treated with herbicides and insecticides have meant the elimination of beneficial insect populations and damage to native plant and animal populations. Farmers who remain involved in animal production pose their own problems, for concentrations of animals produce more manure than can be used by crops on the surrounding lands, resulting in too much phosphorus and nitrogen.

At the same time, our agricultural productivity and consequently low-cost food have affected conservation as well. Dire economic conditions have led a few producers to compromise on conservation practices. The lure of current profits may cause them to eliminate beneficial crop rotations or to engage in practices that erode topsoil or destroy selected soil resources. Farmers renting lands from others may decline to invest in long-term improvements to the land and forgo practices that help preserve soil resources.

The Problem of Soil Erosion

As the foregoing suggests, our conservation practices, central both to the preservation of our agricultural resources and to the beauty of our landscape, are in disarray. Our most notable problem is soil erosion, and many of our conservation efforts have focused on this problem. Ninety percent of our cropland is losing soil above a sustainable rate. According to one estimate, farming practices have cost Iowa one-half its fertile topsoil over the last 150 years.[1] It is estimated that the Minnesota River carries 1.8 tons of sediment through Mankato, Minnesota, each minute.[2]

Damages from erosion and the loss of soil nutrients translate into a yearly economic loss of more than $27 billion.[3] While short-term profitability may lead to practices that exacerbate soil erosion, long-term productivity depends on the preservation of the resource base. We strive for sustainable farming systems that align short-term objectives with long-term productivity and environmental integrity. Erosion threatens these longer-term goals.

Native Americans and other landowners practiced soil-conservation practices long before governments felt a need to become involved. In the 1890s the USDA expressed concern about the abandonment of farmland because of worn-out soils. A 1928 report on soil erosion exposed some of the problems.[4] Researchers calculated that the loss of plant nutrients from excessive erosion was costing American farmers $200 million a year. Nevertheless, the government did little to encourage conservation measures prior to the New Deal legislation of the 1930s because our country had an abundance of resources. The central question in the prevailing philosophy was how to use natural resources, not what might be done to sustain or preserve them.

The economy, too, has influenced the soil-conservation measures our farmers use. Farmers experiencing financial difficulties will find it burdensome to initiate or invest in new conservation measures. Concerned with their financial survival, they are unlikely to practice costly conservation measures. Acknowledging the importance of economics, many governmental regulations have coupled financial assistance with conservation practices in an attempt to encourage farmers to preserve their resources, and producers and governments continue efforts to reconcile production efficiency with the preservation of resources.

Drawing on Regulatory Controls

Facing acknowledged problems of eroding soils, state and federal governments have enacted laws to encourage voluntary stewardship practices. Some farmers have been good caretakers of their resources, and others have not. Many have recognized a need to implement various conservation methods. Others still need to learn more about these matters. Despite myriad regulatory efforts and billions of dollars invested to control erosion, we have not achieved our societal conservation objectives. Farmers continue to engage in erosive practices to obtain short-term profits and survive in the marketplace. More steps are necessary to save our soils, including additional governmental assistance for conservation measures.

Who should pay to curb soil erosion? Policy makers have long wrestled with this question. Because farmers are polluters, some feel that they should pay for the practices and controls needed to circumscribe erosion, with no public funding involved. This approach gives farmers no short-term incentive to adopt conservation practices, however, leaving us with unacceptable erosion and the continued degradation of our soil resources.

Others argue that the central issue is a public resource—the country's soil—and that public investments in soil conservation make economic sense. Experts have concluded that it would cost $8.4 billion per year to limit erosion in the United States to a sustainable rate.[5] Although this is expensive, the annual direct and indirect benefits to society may be greater than $40 billion.

Science has played an important role in the conservation of our natural resources. As we gather more information about the relationships among soils, nutrients, crops, weather, and other components of our environment, we can become better stewards of our natural resources for long-term purposes. One important way to achieve sustainable production and improve our soil is to employ by-products from livestock production, returning to a fertility cycle where manure is used to improve soils for crop production.

The family farm traditionally used manure, with its three macronutrients and other elements, as a production input for multiple crops. Applying manure to the land improved it by expanding the soil's capacity for holding water and retaining nutrients. Today, farms lacking animals apply artificial fertilizers to secure additional nutrients for plant growth. These fertilizers may provide adequate nutrients but lack organic matter and micronutrients important for long-term sustainable production. Without adequate organic matter, soils tend to have inferior physical characteristics and a diminished ability to support beneficial soil organisms.

Thus, animal production cannot be separated from soil conservation and the rural landscape. The lessons of soil conservation—and legislative efforts to foster soil conservation—can provide us foresight for developing responses to the environmental problems associated with AFOs. The number of conservation efforts makes it difficult to describe past efforts, but some general categories can help characterize changes in approaches and philosophy. Conservation activities in our country unfolded in three stages: (1) conservation programs in 1930s New Deal legislation, (2) cultivation versus compensation programs from the 1950s through 1985, and (3) stewardship practices commencing with the 1985 Food Security Act.

Agricultural Conservation in the 1930s

The Great Depression and dust bowl conditions of the 1930s set the stage for radical governmental intervention. The federal New Deal legislation prominently introduced conservation efforts with an emphasis on soil erosion. The government offered landowners technical help and incentives for lessening the harm that agricultural-production activities wrought on common air and water resources. Congress provided funds for soil erosion research in 1933 and created the Soil Conservation Service in 1936. This service evolved into the nation's premier resource conservation agency and shared responsibilities for conservation with the subsequent Agricultural Stabilization and Conservation Service, now known as the Farm Service Agency.

The New Deal legislation served to divert lands from soil-depleting crops until World War II.[6] Farmers were encouraged to reduce acreages of small grains, corn, and cotton by planting soil-conserving crops such as legumes, grass, and pasture crops. All these efforts helped farmers learn how to better manage their soil resources. Participation consisted of voluntary arrangements, however—farmers were not forced to adopt soil-conservation measures. Mandatory regulations for farmers remained well beyond the horizon of legitimate governmental action at the time.

Another development from the 1930s affected soil conservation as well: local soil-conservation districts. Recognizing that enduring conservation required action at the farm level, the USDA drafted a model law to provide for the formation of soil-conservation districts within state governments. By 1947 all fifty states had adopted legislation patterned after the model law.[7] Soil-conservation districts have subsequently served as a vehicle for local farmers and the federal government to implement soil-conservation measures jointly. Anyone who drives along rural roads is familiar with signs noting these districts. Unfortunately, the districts did not guarantee success in preserving soil resources. They have been only partly successful in convincing landowners to initiate practices necessary to reduce erosion to acceptable levels.

Cultivation versus Compensation

The "cultivation versus compensation" stage of conservation activities witnessed federal programs that responded to the boom-and-bust agricultural cycles commencing in the 1950s and ending in 1985. Farmers would cultivate all their lands to maximize production unless some type of governmental compensation program offered an advantageous alternative. This stage commenced after World War II as the war-torn areas of Europe resumed normal agricultural production and our country experienced huge food surpluses. Commodity prices were falling, and a governmen-

tal remedy was recommended. The momentous swings in agricultural-
product demands and surpluses during this period were the driving forces
for new programs that affected the conservation of agricultural resources.

To respond to the problems and reduce surpluses, Congress enacted
the "Soil Bank" program in 1956, compensating farmers for idling acreages. By 1962 this conservation program had removed 25 million acres of
cropland from agricultural production.[8] Perhaps more important, the
program introduced practices and ideas supporting the conservation of
our soil resources. The Soil Bank's conservation practices evolved into
indispensable management practices adopted both here and in the European Union. The Food Security Act of 1985 in part duplicated the Soil Bank
program by setting aside large acreages of agricultural land, and the European Union borrowed its ideas in establishing regulations to reduce
feedstuffs in the 1980s.[9]

Given the Soil Bank's importance in disseminating ideas for improving the rural environment, it is worthwhile to outline the program's conservation practices. The USDA reported the following conservation practices being used under federal programs in the 1960s:

- establishment of a permanent cover
- increasing perennial or biennial legumes
- improvement of permanent cover
- establishment of temporary protective cover
- tree planting
- timber stand improvement
- establishment of sod waterways
- standard terraces
- diversion and spreader terraces
- establishing strip cropping
- tillage operations to control erosion
- stubble mulching
- control of competing shrubs
- development of springs to improve grassland management
- construction of storage-type dams and reservoirs
- lining irrigation ditches
- leveling land to prevent erosion and allow efficient use of
  irrigation
- drainage to permit conservation farming
- lime for conservation cover[10]

We are still advocating and using most of these practices today. A drive through the countryside will confirm the importance of the husbandry techniques that were integral to Soil Bank practices. Farmers are using terracing and strip cropping to preserve soil resources. They have adopted conservation tillage practices to minimize the loss of soil and sow cover crops to control erosion. Farmers plant legumes to add nitrogen to soils. While our federal conservation legislation has changed and financial assistance programs have come and gone, the conservation practices embedded in the Soil Bank program of the 1950s have remained as a foundation for the conservation of our natural resources.

At the same time, the Soil Bank program is now considered less than a success. It lacked details that would have advanced the application of conservation responses to the most egregious situations. Because some farmers did not participate, erosion continued to plague their fields. Rather than concentrate on acreages subject to erosion, farmers signed up their least productive acres. Moreover, because the idled acreages led to lower total yields, individual farmers often sought to recoup lost yields by intensifying production efforts on lands not in the Soil Bank program. Farmers might apply more fertilizer or forgo soil-conserving crops to maintain yields and income. Occasionally they introduced erosive practices on the other acreages. Alternatively, they would shift production to alternative crops that the set-aside program did not cover, creating potential surpluses of those crops.

The program's greatest infirmity, however, was the temporary nature of many of these conservation practices. Farmers could discontinue the practices at any time. Indeed, most of this acreage returned to crop production when economic forces led farmers to return to intensive production practices in the 1970s.[11] Burgeoning international markets resulted in outlets for more crop products. We feared food shortages, so farmers were again encouraged to plant fencerow to fencerow. Increased feedstuff prices led farmers to initiate new plantings on marginal lands, cease conservation practices, and intensify cultivation on other lands. As expected, greater soil erosion generally accompanied these renewed agricultural activities. The American countryside reverted to the food-production engine that had been so important during World War II. Although the ideals of the Soil Bank Program supported the long-term conservation of our agricultural resources, its ephemeral nature prevented it from yielding the intended results.

Stewardship and the Food Security Act of 1985

When it was clear that our country had sufficient supplies of agricultural commodities, the Food Security Act of 1985 ushered in the third stage: the implementation of stewardship practices. This act contained fresh, enterprising provisions on environmental protection and on conservation measures for private lands. Although this act, too, failed to mandate conservation measures on specific types of cropland, it provided farmers with incentives to adopt environmental stewardship practices. Voluntary provisions to preserve fragile soils from production, retain swamplands, and place highly erodible lands in set-aside programs were the cornerstones of a new conservation ethic. Cross-compliance measures proscribed federal subsidies to farms that failed to carry out appropriate conservation measures. This stage has evolved to include programs and efforts to respond to the public's desire to safeguard natural resources for current and future generations.

Sodbuster and Swampbuster Provisions

The "sodbuster" provisions of the Food Security Act addressed erosion problems occurring on highly erodible lands. The loss of good topsoil, long known to be a problem, diminishes future agricultural yields and causes environmental problems through the siltation of streams and rivers. Because highly erodible fields accounted for 58 percent of all cropland erosion, these provisions yielded noteworthy benefits. In effect, the 1985 conservation provisions were a long overdue recognition that there is no right to destroy the soil.

Under sodbuster, eligibility for governmental payments requires the adoption and application of a conservation compliance plan for fields consisting of predominantly highly erodible land (nearly one-quarter of all agricultural land).[12] After fifty years of conservation efforts, our federal government finally found the political willpower to go beyond a completely voluntary program. Sodbuster was not compulsory, but its cross-compliance provisions forced farmers who wanted government subsidies to develop a conservation plan. The implementation of these plans achieved dramatic results. Yearly erosion rates on highly erodible land dropped from an average of 17.4 tons to 5.8 tons per acre.[13]

Wetlands and swamplands were viewed as meriting special attention as well. Despite many suggestions for ways to preserve wetlands, no meaningful response had emerged. The Food Security Act set forth a "swampbuster" provision to reduce the conversion of wetlands to cropland, chiefly by denying subsidies to farmers who destroy wetlands. Again, the incentive is purely financial. Property owners may drain or destroy wetlands as they choose, but those who do so become ineligible for USDA payments.

Swampbuster thus fails to affect anyone not participating in federal commodity, loan, or other programs. In addition, various exemptions and mitigations temper the swampbuster ineligibility provisions in some circumstances. Finally, swampbuster does not apply to developers or nonfarmers, so that wetlands may still be lost to development. Governments must therefore look beyond swampbuster to preserve our nation's wetlands more effectively, and other regulations have been adopted to advance this goal.

The Conservation Reserve Program

Although the sodbuster and swampbuster provisions of the Food Security Act were significant—and have made an explicit contribution to our nation's conservation efforts—the act's most celebrated component was the Conservation Reserve Program (CRP). The CRP set aside agricultural acreage to reduce production, conserve soil, and improve water quality. The major conservation goal was to control erosion by removing highly erodible land from commodity production.

Farmers applied to their county Agricultural Stabilization and Conservation Service Office to enroll lands in the CRP. In this application the farmers would indicate the annual rental payment they would require for participating in the program. Once accepted into the program, lands were enrolled for ten years and could not be used for commodity production during this period. In return, the farmer received an annual rental payment from the government. The CRP's goal was to remove about 13 percent of our nation's total cropland from production. The initial CRP contracts between landowners and the government were signed in 1986. From 1986 to 1994 more than 370,000 landowners enrolled 36.4 million acres in the program.[14] The CRP became a major avenue for governmental infusions of money into the agricultural sector in the late 1980s and early 1990s.

Although the CRP was not without environmental benefits, the implementation of the program has received criticism. Our federal government did not heed the lessons provided by the Soil Bank program of the 1950s, once again failing to target the most erodible land: the government's procedure allowed farmers to set aside their least productive land, not the most erodible. Moreover, experts have argued that the CRP failed economically—that, since cheaper solutions existed, it was too expensive for the conservation gains achieved. One researcher suggested that financial subsidies requiring alternative production practices could have reduced crop erosion to acceptable levels for most of the enrolled land. Such financial subsidies might have cost about $200 million, a tenth of the $2 billion spent under the CRP.[15]

Additional Stewardship Efforts

Legacies from the 1985 Food Security Act continue to provide basic regulatory provisions to encourage soil conservation. Subsequent adjustments have added positive stewardship provisions to enhance performance. As agriculture's percentage of our gross national product shrinks, and Americans become accustomed to plentiful food supplies, we have increased our efforts to conserve resources through more meaningful conservation programs.

One important development has been more focused efforts to achieve conservation objectives, such as the Wetlands Reserve Program adopted by Congress in 1990. This program enrolled nearly one million acres of wetlands for habitat protection and water-quality benefits. In 1996 the "Freedom to Farm" Act dismantled existing farm commodity programs. The act freed up acreages that had been enrolled in the CRP program but retained measures to conserve highly erodible land and wetlands. The act was meant to repeal traditional farm programs that encouraged overproduction of major agricultural commodities,[16] but it was not successful. Falling farm prices and incomes led Congress to pass a new farm bill in 2002.

Conservation initiatives adopted in 1996 provided farmers with technical assistance, education, cost sharing, and incentive payments. Three types of practices that conserve, protect, or improve soil and water qualified for financial assistance: (1) land-management practices involving nutrient management, manure management, tillage or residue management, strip cropping, contour farming, and wildlife-habitat management; (2) vegetative practices embracing contour grass strips, filter strips, tree planting, and permanent wildlife habitat; and (3) structural practices encompassing animal waste-management facilities and grassed waterways. Special federal-state programs provided farmers who adopted specified conservation practices with financial incentives to take land out of agricultural production.

Future Conservation Efforts

Over the past forty years our federal and state governments have committed billions of dollars to preserve our soil and water resources. At the end of the twentieth century, 3 million farms and ranches had placed 2 billion acres in soil conservation districts.[17] Approximately 30 million acres were in federal conservation programs. Governments at all levels were spending nearly $1 billion per year for conservation programs.[18] Yet agriculture remained the number-one non-point-source polluter of our nation's rivers and streams. Clearly, we need to do more to contain erosion and other sources of contamination. Given the damages associated with non-point-source pollution, our federal government will continue to experiment with new programs and approaches. Past programs suggest three options for approaching these problems.

First, we might follow the practices and programs set forth in the federal agricultural-conservation programs, relying mainly on voluntary controls and incentives. This approach includes disincentives, such as being disqualified from other federal benefits. The desire to provide farmers flexibility in using their property means we will continue to rely on such voluntary approaches, but these may not suffice for our long-term conservation objectives. Without regulations bearing the force of law, we cannot compel farmers and property owners to adopt conservation practices to abate non-point-source pollution. Financial incentives can sustain conservation measures, but the conservation practices do not survive the termination of the inevitably temporary governmental funding programs.

Thus, policy makers may decide to forgo temporary programs and move to the second option, more lasting stewardship practices under a more heavy-handed approach. Governments might emulate point-source pollution regulations consisting of mandatory controls and prohibitions. For egregious situations, such as contamination from animal waste, new regulations might prohibit activities or require the further treatment of animal waste to reduce contamination. State and local governments may choose to accord society additional protection by enacting mandatory controls to address deplorable conditions, such as nitrogen and phosphorus pollution. Environmental requirements may compel farmers to end long-standing business activities, and the high costs of compliance may drive animal production from some regions. The potential exists for environmental policy to dictate agricultural policy and programs.

The third approach combines the previous two options. The distinctions are profound—especially due to the high costs associated with mandatory performance and enforcement controls and the precarious financial situation of many agricultural producers. Farm operators know the options and the stakes—they are striving to do better at voluntarily controlling pollution in the hope of thwarting more onerous controls. Nevertheless, market factors continue to influence farmers, leading some to forgo sufficient voluntary practices. Indeed, our history suggests that the voluntary conservation model cannot meet our society's environment goals.

NOTES

1. David Pimentel et al., "Environmental and Economic Costs of Soil Erosion and Conservation Benefits," *Science* 267 (1995): 1117–21.

2. Dana L. Jackson, "The Farm as a Natural Habitat," in *The Farm as a Natural Habitat: Reconnecting Food Systems with Ecosystems,* ed. Dana L. Jackson and Laura L. Jackson (Washington, D.C.: Island, 2002), 15.

3. Pimentel et al., "Environmental and Economic Costs," 1117–21.

4. H. H. Bennett and W. R. Chapline, *Soil Erosion: A National Menace,* USDA circular no. 33 (Washington, D.C.: USDA, 1928).

5. Pimentel et al., "Environmental and Economic Costs," 1121.

6. Harold G. Halcrow, Earl O. Heady, and Melvin L. Cotner, *Soil Conservation, Policies, Institutions, and Incentives* (Ankeny, Iowa: Soil Conservation Society, 1982), 7.

7. Ibid., 8.

8. U.S. Department of Agriculture, *Agricultural Statistics 1962* (Washington, D.C.: USDA, 1962), 639.

9. Margaret R. Grossman and Wim Brussaard, *Agrarian Land Law in the Western World: Essays about Agrarian Land Policy and Regulation in Twelve Countries of the Western World* (New York: CABI, 1992).

10. USDA, *Agricultural Statistics 1962,* 642–47.

11. Clive Potter, *Against the Grain: Agri-Environmental Reform in the United States and the European Union* (Wallingford, U.K.: CAB International, 1998), 13.

12. Linda A. Malone, "Conservation at the Crossroads: Reauthorization of the 1985 Farm Bill," *Virginia Environmental Law Journal* 8 (1989): 215–33.

13. J. Dixon Esseks et al., "Policy Lessons from a Quasi-Regulatory Conservation Program," in *Soil and Water Conservation,* ed. Ted L. Napier et al. (Boca Raton, Fla.: CRC, 1999), 109–25.

14. U.S. Department of Agriculture, *Agricultural Statistics 1997* (Washington, D.C.: USDA, 1997), XII-1.

15. Jim Sinner, "Soil Conservation: We Can Get More for Our Tax Dollars," *Choices* (2d Quarter 1990): 10.

16. Jason Waanders, "Comment: Growing a Greener Future? USDA and Natural Resource Conservation," *Environmental Law* 29 (1999): 235–78.

17. U.S. Department of Agriculture, *Agricultural Statistics 1999* (Washington, D.C.: USDA, 1999), XII-21.

18. Ibid., XII-20.

Animal waste lagoon at a concentrated swine operation (Natural Resources Conservation Service)

Two confined sows with piglets (U.S. Department of Agriculture)

Confined hogs at a grow-out facility (Natural Resources Conservation Service)

Confined chickens in a roomful of battery cages (Farm Sanctuary)

Cattle stockyard containing approximately 36,000 animals (photo courtesy Dr. Brent Auvermann, Texas A&M University System, Amarillo)

Freestall dairy (photo courtesy Dr. S. Mukhtar, Department of Biological and Agricultural Engineering, Texas A&M University)

Broiler houses for confined chickens (photo courtesy University of Georgia)

Confined broilers (photo courtesy University of Georgia)

8   Odors and Nuisance Law

The area around my family's farm was home to various farm activities. When I was a teen, our closest neighbor's son finished his B.S. degree in agriculture and returned to the family farm, determined to expand operations and create a two-family farm out of the meager holding. He built two state-of-the-art chicken houses and brought in thousands of chicks to raise into broilers. The chicken houses were not close to our house, but we could see them through the trees. We did not consider them a nuisance—after all, we lived in the country. In fact, my maternal grandfather was raising thousands of chickens just a few miles away. For a couple of years my brother and I took Dad's tractor and manure spreader to my grandfather's chicken barn to collect free chicken manure for our 4-H vegetable garden.

Still, neither cow manure nor our familiarity with chickens completely prepared us for the smell that occasionally emanated from our neighbor's chicken houses. From time to time he experienced problems with his watering system. The culprit was a defective overflow valve that allowed water to flood part of the chicken house, creating a loathsome mess of wet poultry litter. Our neighbor would eventually remove the wet litter, usually spreading it on fields, and the smells would dissipate after a few days.

> *Once, however, he simply deposited the sodden litter in a pile beside the chicken house. We could see the pile from our front yard. It remained in view for weeks, dispensing its horrible smells throughout the neighborhood. Fortunately the prevailing winds tended to move the odors away from our farm—only occasional shifts of wind brought the smell our way. Others were less lucky. Our daily schoolbus ride gave us an idea of the odors afflicting our poor neighbors on the leeward side. Neighbors should not be forced to endure such stenches from improper agricultural operations.*

Excrement stinks, and although the public may continue to support conservation programs even when they fall short of expectations, it has little patience with malodorous neighbors.[1] Whether the stench is coming from industry, municipal wastewater-treatment facilities, or farms, most perceive such annoyances as unfair. Citizens have moved beyond mere discussion to petition legislatures for relief. And they are turning to the courts as well, using common law to sue those responsible. Under nuisance law, a court balances the equities, deferring to majority rule to enjoin a nuisance activity.

AFOs are prime targets for such lawsuits. Manure and other waste accompanying livestock production often create offensive smells. Public and private nuisance law lets neighbors take action to end the disagreeable activity. Neighbors can petition courts for legal remedies, which include court orders requiring the offenders to adopt technology to abate the irritants and injunctions requiring them to stop the activities altogether.

As livestock operations increase in size, the offensive smells emanating from them become more widely noticeable. Most livestock producers attempt to abate the offending odors, so that neighbors do not resort to nuisance law to enjoin the objectionable activity. On the whole, farmers strive to minimize the offensiveness of their activities, whether by plowing manure into the soil soon after applying it to a field or by limiting their use of noisy equipment late at night to fields away from neighboring residences.

Right-to-Farm Protection

In the late 1960s concern about new neighbors using nuisance law to stop agricultural activities led agricultural interest groups to advance anti-nuisance legislation, which came to be called "right-to-farm" laws. Basically, these laws allow farmers to continue with bothersome activities if they were operating before the complainants moved into the area. These laws do not resolve the conflicts; they simply alter the boundaries, modestly shifting the balance of competing property rights. These laws thus protect some agricultural activities, although neighbors can still employ nuisance law to stop objectionable practices and anticipated nuisances in other situations.

Recognizing agriculture's importance, all states have enacted right-to-farm laws to curb nuisance litigation. Right-to-farm laws resemble zoning provisions in that both restrict the rights of property owners by circumscribing uses of land within a certain area. Zoning laws straightforwardly delineate districts in which particular land uses and activities are proscribed, for example, barring businesses from residential districts. Right-to-farm laws prevent persons with new land uses for which an agricultural operation is objectionable from employing nuisance law to enjoin existing agricultural operations, essentially denying them the protection of nuisance law. More specifically, most right-to-farm laws protect farmers' existing investments in their agricultural operations via a "coming to the nuisance" doctrine: neighbors who come to an agricultural nuisance may not sue.[2] The typical scenario involves a residential subdivision built near existing farms; a few years later the new neighbors attempt to use nuisance law to enjoin some farming activity they find objectionable. Right-to-farm laws prohibit such suits.

Right-to-farm laws are often crucially important to livestock producers. Raising animals involves manure, and manure smells bad. The American public is generally unfamiliar with animal production and does not fully realize the difficulties farmers face in controlling odors and disposing of manure. Many Americans do not adequately appreciate the value of using manure as a fertilizer. Even persons disposed to environmental goals are hard pressed to accept smelly manure. Right-to-farm laws, however, have sufficiently protected such agricultural activities from nuisance lawsuits, so that farmers there first can continue their operations.

Obviously, as with any broad category of legislation, there are exceptions. No two state right-to-farm laws are the same. In fact, some diverged markedly from the generalized example. Some right-to-farm laws protect only specific activities, require the creation of agricultural districts, or apply solely to those who use generally accepted agricultural management practices. A few right-to-farm laws, however, favor agriculture to the detriment of other landowners. As might be expected, such injustice makes these laws controversial. For most laws, however, the fundamental question is this: why should established legal principles of nuisance be changed solely for agriculture? Codifying a coming-to-the nuisance defense may provide one answer, but most laws still show favoritism to agriculture by not protecting other commercial or business interests in similar circumstances.

Inception Date

To examine an operation or activity under a traditional right-to-farm law, we first must determine when it began. Right-to-farm laws were intended to protect the investments of existing operations from new land uses and nuisance actions, and most such laws clearly limit their protection to operations that started prior to surrounding land uses. The date the operation or activity began is therefore crucial. Generally, an agricultural operation that has been in business for more than one year prior to new land uses is afforded protection from nuisance lawsuits. Property owners with land uses that preceded agricultural activities, however, can employ nuisance law to obtain relief from an objectionable farm activity.

Farmers do not always appreciate this limitation and often have a false sense of security under their right-to-farm laws. Several cases have involved farmers who failed to understand this. In one case involving the construction of an egg farm in a pasture, residential neighbors sued the farm to eliminate the flies and offensive odors generated by the poultry.[3] The neighbors claimed the farm was a nuisance, and asked the court to shut down its operation. The court enjoined the farm under nuisance law, ruling that the right-to-farm law did not apply because the egg farm was built after the residents had moved into their homes.

A case involving a private summer camp ended similarly.[4] The camp had existed for sixty years, and the neighboring farmers had been raising hogs for fifteen years. The camp owners requested injunctive relief from the smell of the hogs, which were confined within ten feet of the camp's grounds. The farmers argued that the right-to-farm law protected their agricultural activities, but the court disagreed. Because the camp preceded the farm operation, the right-to-farm law could not serve as a defense. Rather, the farm was ruled a nuisance.

Prerequisites and Activities Covered

Right-to-farm laws have prerequisites concerning agricultural practices. Some states require that agricultural producers be in an agricultural district or that farms conform to a municipal master plan before they qualify for nuisance protection. In addition, the law may require that the activity at issue be conducted in accordance with generally accepted agricultural practices. Other provisions may exempt improper and negligent agricultural activities from protection.

Right-to-farm laws differ considerably on the activities they cover. Some laws limit coverage to farms and farming operations, whereas others cover the manufacturing of animal feed and roadside markets. Generally, right-to-farm laws cover the growing and harvesting of crops; the feeding, breeding, and management of livestock; and other agricultural and horticultural uses of land.

This variability means that defendants must examine their individual states' laws closely to determine whether they protect any particular activity. For example, an agricultural manufacturing facility's wastewater lagoons were found to fall outside a right-to-farm law.[5] The court reasoned that the law covered only the marketing activities of agricultural operations involved in the production of plants and animals. Since the lagoons were part of a manufacturing facility owned by a corporation that was not involved in production, the right-to-farm protection against nuisance actions was not applicable. In another case a manufacturer of utility poles from untreated logs raised a right-to-farm defense to a nuisance claim.[6] The court ruled that the manufacturing activity occurred in an industrial area and thus could not be characterized as agricultural. The right-to-farm law did not apply.

Right-to-farm laws are commonly limited to commercial activities. Most right-to-farm laws were not intended to allow hobbyists or non-farmers to engage in activities that neighbors find objectionable, manifesting this intention by excluding small or part-time operators from the laws' protection. For example, one right-to-farm law specifically excludes operations of less than ten contiguous acres with an anticipated annual gross income of less than $10,000.[7]

Permitted Expansion

The expansion of an existing agricultural operation poses a difficult issue under most right-to-farm laws. To remain competitive, agricultural operations must grow and expand. Right-to-farm laws thus must allow such developments if they are to afford meaningful protection to agricultural producers.

Simultaneously, unlimited expansion can be unfair to neighbors. Existing neighbors may not mind the production of crops or a small-scale livestock operation, but the introduction of animals to a crop farm or a marked increase of animals can significantly alter attitudes. Neighbors should not have to bear the increased inconveniences generated by an expanded operation.

Such conflicts have posed difficulties for legislatures addressing this issue. Some legislatures have overtly favored agriculture by allowing unlimited expansion. Under such laws, a farmer may be able to expand an operation exponentially and still qualify for whatever protection was available to the earlier facility. Other legislatures have recognized that some expansion is necessary, but so too are limits to the protection. Under one approach, only a percentage of the expansion can qualify for right-to-farm protection.[8] Another excludes large operations, such as those with more than 1,000 swine or 2,500 cattle. Alternatively, some right-to-farm laws limit expansion to preclude excessive noise, dust, and odors.[9]

Finally, a few right-to-farm laws simply do not cover expansion. These laws specifically state that they apply only when there is no significant change in type of operation and the operation would not have been a nuisance when it began in that locality.[10]

Technological and Production Changes

To survive, agricultural operations must not only expand; they must also adopt new technology and new production methods. Farming is not static. Inventions lead to new machinery and methods for producing farm products, and farmers must be able to incorporate these inventions. Vagaries of crop markets also may force a farmer to make changes in production. The ability to make such changes and retain protection against nuisance lawsuits is important to farmers. Therefore, they have sought the protection of right-to-farm laws for these developments.

Some right-to-farm laws include the adoption of new technology. One such law covers "new activities, practices, equipment and procedures consistent with technological development within the agricultural industry."[11] Under these provisions, farmers can adopt new technology without losing the protection of the right-to-farm law.

Determining whether a right-to-farm law protects new technology generally requires scrutiny of the law's provisions. In a controversy involving a new poultry housing design accompanied by a change from the application of dry manure to wet manure, a court carefully examined the right-to-farm law's provisions concerning environmental degradation. The court determined that although the law permits minor odor changes and minimal degradation of the environment, it does not protect substantial degradation. Right-to-farm laws, it ruled, are not intended to serve "as an un-fettered license for farmers to alter the environment of their locale."[12]

Right-to-farm laws generally do not protect operations that change production activities. For example, the construction of a hog-confine-ment building and the production of hogs on a farm was not protected from a nuisance action by an existing neighbor.[13] Because the nuisance resulted from changes on the farm rather than new neighboring land uses, the farm did not qualify for the nuisance protection.

In another case, a change from grain farming to a hog-raising opera-tion was found to constitute a significant and hence unprotected change.[14] The same court, however, felt that the law protected changes involving increases in the number of hogs raised on a farm. Thus, the court permitted expansion under the law but did not approve a new pro-duction activity.

Compliance with Other Laws

Many people feel they should be able to buy environmental quality. They acquire expensive homes in attractive subdivisions to avoid commercial and industrial areas or move to the country to escape urban problems. Such individuals often feel that they should not have to endure the smells emitted from a livestock facility or manure spread on a nearby field, and they may turn to the legal system for relief.

Most right-to-farm laws do not obviate the requirements of other laws, nor do they affect other causes of action in tort, such as actions in negli-gence or trespass. That is, if the activities violate other legal provisions, the right-to-farm laws do not offer protection to the operation or operator.

Many right-to-farm laws specifically exempt negligent or improper operations from their protection, explicitly retaining common-law ac-tions in negligence. Other laws simply say that they do not affect any other right to sue for damages.

Agricultural producers remain subject to zoning ordinances, building codes, and other local and state laws as well. If a municipality zones an area to eliminate animals that could cause health problems, an existing farm operation may be forced out of business despite the nuisance pro-tection of a state right-to-farm law. Compliance with environmental laws is another question that has received attention. Most right-to-farm laws do not interfere with environmental laws or pollution legislation.[15] For example, livestock producers must comply with legislation governing clean water and the disposal of manure.

In addition, farmers remain subject to public health and safety regulations, including local legislation, which citizens may pass to curtail health hazards created by flies, vermin, and manure waste. At the state level, such regulations include setback requirements to protect properties near AFOs from odors. Some states require CAFOs to be located more than one mile from selected property uses to alleviate nuisances. Counties generally have authority to enhance public health through regulations limiting CAFOs under their health ordinances.

Constitutional Prohibition of "Takings"

The "just compensation clause" of the Constitution's Fifth Amendment requires payment if the government forces some people to bear public burdens. Whenever the government "takes" property rights for a public use, compensation is owed.[16] Whether a taking has occurred, however, depends on the particular circumstances of the case. State constitutions have similar provisions on takings. Any governmental action that operates to take an individual's property must be accompanied by compensation to the property owner. All takings of property, both permanent and temporary, require compensation under the just compensation clause.[17]

At the same time, government has the power to enact laws and ordinances for our benefit. This is why we have governments—they exercise their "police powers" for the public good, whether via a speed limit to make our roads safer or through a zoning ordinance to prevent land-use conflicts. Different individuals may be less than pleased with some of these laws. Smokers may be opposed to the no-smoking rules in restaurants and government buildings, and business owners may feel we have too many safety and environmental regulations.

A right-to-farm law is subject to the same constitutional limitations as are other exercises of a state's police power. The question is whether an action by the state constitutes a use of the police power to sustain health and safety or is a regulatory taking that requires compensation. Laws and other governmental regulations that substantially promote public health, safety, or general welfare are permitted as justified police powers. Compensation is due, however, if a governmental action is a taking. For example, overly stringent regulations precluding the use of property in a floodplain may constitute a taking. If the action goes beyond merely restricting the use of property, it is a taking.[18]

By granting farmers—and sometimes businesses—the right to continue with existing objectionable activities despite changes in nearby land uses, right-to-farm laws often lessen the value of neighboring real estate. What happens if a neighborhood changes, perhaps with new residential neighborhoods being added in an expanding urban area? Despite changes caused by urban growth, persons moving next to a hog farm protected by a right-to-farm law cannot do anything about the stinky farm. Notwithstanding the overwhelming transformation of an area and the dominance of residential property uses, the farm gets to stay. The stench wins.

Of course, the reason for adopting right-to-farm laws was to protect existing farms. Many farmers have spent years investing in their business operations. Why should new neighbors be able to use nuisance law to force them to give up their livelihoods? Why should farmers' buildings and other investments be rendered valueless, or nearly so? The neighbors who moved into the area knew about the hogs yet decided to live there anyway. If people elect to come to a nuisance, let them do so.

Courts have noted that right-to-farm laws reduce the rights of neighbors, diminish the value of neighboring properties, and create easements (rights to use another's land) or servitudes (benefits for a property owner) over neighboring properties. Yet creating easements or servitudes is hardly a new occurrence; many governmental regulations do this. Zoning ordinances often prevent owners from using their property for a more profitable use. Many a suburban residential property owner tries to open a little business at home only to discover that a zoning ordinance prohibits it. Persons and businesses in historic districts routinely discover that an ordinance bars them from making exterior changes to buildings. These ordinances are valid under a local government's police powers, even though they reduce the regulated properties' value.

The Iowa Takings Challenge

In *Bormann v. Board of Supervisors* plaintiffs before the Iowa Supreme Court argued that a right-to-farm law went too far in reducing the property rights of neighbors.[19] The court agreed, ruling that the egregious infringement of neighbors' rights embodied an unconstitutional taking violating the federal and the state's constitutions. In favoring the private property rights of neighbors, the *Bormann* court ruled against overbearing right-to-farm laws and industrial agriculture. Right-to-farm laws usurp property rights of neighbors, and as the *Bormann* decision indicates, any law that takes too many property rights from neighbors is a taking.

The right-to-farm law considered by the *Bormann* court, however, did not have a coming-to-the-nuisance doctrine. Unlike most such laws, the defective Iowa law granted antinuisance protection to agricultural producers who commenced new activities that would be a nuisance with respect to current land uses.

An example will illustrate the scope of the Iowa law before its annulment by the Iowa Supreme Court. Consider a crop farm in a newly formed agricultural area that is subsequently developed into an objectionable AFO. Would neighbors be able to successfully maintain a nuisance lawsuit given the protection proffered by the Iowa law? The answer seems to be no. Rather than consider when an agricultural operation or AFO was established, the Iowa law simply eliminated farming operations in an agricultural area from the nuisance category. Operations could change, AFOs could be developed, and the antinuisance provisions of the defective Iowa law shielded the operations from neighbors' nuisance lawsuits.

Right-to-farm laws were not intended to interfere with the property rights of longtime rural residents. They were not meant to allow the construction of new, objectionable facilities in rural areas. Nuisance protection was provided only against new neighboring land uses. Existing neighbors possess the right to use nuisance law against agricultural facilities that are a nuisance. If an operation starts a new activity that is a nuisance, such as changing from a crop farm to an AFO, it should not be protected by a right-to-farm law.

Because right-to-farm laws with the coming-to-the-nuisance doctrine do not offer protection for future agricultural activities, they do not embrace a servitude or easement over existing land uses of the type considered in the *Bormann* case. Rather, these laws create restrictions that can be justified as permissible regulations serving legitimate public purposes. Thus, the *Bormann* decision does not presage the end to the nuisance protection afforded by most right-to-farm laws. Other states' laws simply incorporate a common-law provision, the coming-to-the-nuisance doctrine, to provide special protection against nuisance actions for qualifying agricultural operations.

Provisions That May Be Challenged

The *Bormann* ruling, while binding on courts in Iowa, does not apply in other states. Nevertheless, the importance of agriculture in Iowa and the respect we have for state supreme court decisions make the precedent significant. The *Bormann* ruling spells trouble for laws that try to protect future nuisance activities. Any law that fails to limit protection to the coming-to-the-nuisance doctrine is subject to challenge.

Given these parameters on takings challenges, what provisions in state right-to-farm laws are most likely to be challenged? These laws may overstep permissible regulation in at least two circumstances. First, provisions containing broad permission for expansion and new technology may face challenges. By permitting new or expanded activities, such laws basically forgo the coming-to-the-nuisance doctrine. Thus, the right-to-farm law may unfairly interfere with neighbors' property rights and constitute a regulatory taking.

For example, consider Georgia's right-to-farm law, which does adopt a coming-to-the-nuisance doctrine by limiting protection to situations where conditions around the agricultural facility change.[20] However, the law includes a provision that permits expansion and new technology: "If the physical facilities of the agricultural operation are subsequently expanded or new technology adopted, the established date of operation for each change is not a separately and independently established date of operation and the commencement of the expanded operation does not divest the agricultural operation of a previously established date of operation."[21] This "relation-back" provision thus allows agricultural facilities to commence new nuisance activities when expanding or adopting new technology. Even though nothing physically invades the neighboring properties, the objectionable activity may be so onerous that a court could rule it a regulatory taking.

Second, right-to-farm laws that incorporate certain limitations may face challenges. Consider, for example, Pennsylvania's right-to-farm law.[22] A court interpreted this law as establishing a one-year statute of limitation.[23] Neighbors who want to bring a nuisance action must do so within one year of the commencement of the offensive activity. The one-year statute of limitation thus provides a permanent defense against certain nuisance actions. The more permanent the nuisance protection afforded by a law, however, the more likely that a trial court will see the law as a taking. The nuisance protection granted by Pennsylvania law may so undermine the rights of existing neighbors that it effects a taking.

Anticipated Nuisances from Livestock Facilities

The public's fear of odors from livestock facilities has resulted in peremptory actions. Two recent lawsuits exemplify the development of nuisance law to cover anticipated nuisances. Under this doctrine, activities can be enjoined as nuisances whenever their existence in the proposed location can be anticipated to constitute a nuisance. This means that a landowner can be sued under nuisance law during preparations to open or expand a facility, before any animals arrive. A state's right-to-farm law would not offer any protection because the facility does not antedate the conflicting land uses.

One relevant case involved a nuisance action against a proposed hog facility.[24] The neighbors sought to stop the construction of a 1,345–acre commercial hog-breeding facility, using a state law that allowed courts to restrain the completion of a facility or an operation bound to create a nuisance. To assemble evidence that the proposed facility would in fact constitute a nuisance, the neighbors secured testimony from a representative of the facility's future owner and operator. The representative testified that the facility would house up to 22,800 hogs at any given time; that the feces, urine, and other waste would drain into concrete pits under each building; that anaerobic and aerobic lagoons would be used to break down the waste; and that the liquefied mixture would be pumped to and distributed over various spray fields. Further testimony showed that the structures, holding pits, lagoons, and animals would send constant, unpleasant odors within a half-mile of the facility. The representative even admitted that, several times a year, persons two to three miles away would smell the stench.

The court also heard testimony that the proposed facility was not being located in North Carolina because of past environmental violations and incidents. The neighbors presented testimony from an expert environmental engineer and a geochemist who stated that the lagoons would produce certain irritating and foul-smelling gasses. Moreover, they said, waste from the facility would likely infiltrate and contaminate groundwater at and around the site.

The court found sufficient evidence that the construction and operation of the proposed hog-breeding facility would constitute a nuisance. Although the mere apprehension of injury and damage is insufficient for granting relief under nuisance law, the court found that these neighbors had proved more. There was a reasonable certainty that irreparable harm and damage would occur from the operation of an otherwise lawful business.

The second case is similar.[25] The defendant was establishing a swine nursery and confinement facility. The plaintiffs were neighbors who were concerned about contamination of the aquifer and odors. The court interpreted the state's law as allowing injunctive relief for both anticipated nuisance and trespass claims.

These cases show that communities and neighbors can be proactive in limiting the development of large CAFOs. Citizens have recourse against objectionable odors and other nuisances and, by bringing action against an anticipated nuisance, can protect themselves from odors from new CAFOs.

A Question of Too Much Protection

The general perception is that right-to-farm laws provide excessive nuisance protection for agricultural activities. Common-law nuisance is based on balancing equities. If common law can successfully handle disputes concerning nuisances from commercial and industrial land uses, why can't it work for agriculture?

Especially egregious are a few right-to-farm provisions that allow farmers to expand facilities or change activities with impunity from nuisance lawsuits. But most right-to-farm laws do not provide absolute protection from nuisance lawsuits. Instead, they simply establish a coming-to-the-nuisance doctrine. This provides farmers a statutory legal defense analogous to one recognized by common law. A person who voluntarily moves next to an activity should not be able to subsequently complain that the activity ought to be prohibited as a nuisance.

Moreover, farm neighbors are not defenseless. Neighbors who resided next to an operation before the right-to-farm law was adopted retain their nuisance rights. Even new neighbors have rights under other laws and regulations that offer avenues to abate unacceptable behavior. Because right-to-farm laws limit only nuisance law, citizens can circumvent the laws by petitioning state and local governments for other legislation to address problems posed by agricultural neighbors. Except in Michigan, right-to-farm laws do not interfere with local ordinances, zoning provisions, environmental proscriptions, and health laws. Finally, citizens may have further remedies under an anticipatory nuisance or the constitutional protection against takings.

NOTES

1. Terence J. Centner, *Legal Structures Governing Animal Waste Management,* White Papers on Animal Agriculture and the Environment (Raleigh, N.C.: National Center for Manure and Animal Waste Management, 2002), ch. 15.

2. Neil D. Hamilton, *A Producer's Legal Guide to: Nuisance, Land Use Control, and Environmental Law* (Des Moines, Iowa: Drake University Law Center, 1992), 21.

3. Herrin v. Opatut, 281 S.E.2d 575 (Ga. 1981).

4. Mayes v. Tabor, 334 S.E.2d 489 (N.C. App. 1985).

5. Knoff v. American Crystal Sugar Co., 380 N.W.2d 313 (N.D. 1986).

6. Roberts v. Southern Wood Piedmont Company, 328 S.E.2d 391 (Ga. App. 1985).

7. *Pennsylvania Statutes,* title 3, §952.

8. *Minnesota Statutes* §561.19.

9. *Florida Statutes* §823.14(5).

10. *Indiana Statutes Annotated* §34-19-1-4.

11. *Pennsylvania Statutes,* title 3, §952.

12. Pasco County v. Tampa Farm Service, Inc., 573 So.2d 909, 912 (Fla. App. 1990).

13. Flansburgh v. Coffey, 370 N.W.2d 127 (Neb. 1985).

14. Laux v. Chopin Land Associates, Inc., 550 N.E.2d 100 (Ind. App. 1990).

15. Margaret R. Grossman and Thomas G. Fischer, "Protecting the Right to Farm: Statutory Limits on Nuisance Actions against the Farmer," *Wisconsin Law Review* (1983): 95–165.

16. Penn Central Transportation Co. v. City of New York, 438 U.S. 104, 123 (1978).

17. First Evangelical Lutheran Church v. County of Los Angeles, 482 U.S. 304, 318 (1987).

18. Penn Central Transportation Co. v. City of New York, 438 U.S. at 123–25 (1978).

19. Bormann v. Board of Supervisors, 584 N.W.2d 309, 321 (Iowa 1998).

20. *Georgia Code Annotated* §41-1-7.

21. Ibid.

22. *Pennsylvania Statutes,* title 3, §952.

23. Horne v. Haladay, 728 A.2d 728 (Pa. Super. Ct. 1999).

24. Superior Farm Management v. Montgomery, 270 Ga. 615 (1999).

25. Rutter v. Carroll's Foods of the Midwest, Inc., 50 F. Supp.2d 876 (W.D. Iowa 1999).

9   Pesticide Contamination Precedents: Liability and Management

Although cows and grapes were my family's main sources of income, the vegetable garden was a source of great pride. With Dad as our adviser, my brother and I joined forces to raise a huge garden and sold our produce in the fall at a roadside stand. Each year we planned our garden around two primary events to earn funds for our future college education—the county fair, with its prize money, and our fall stand. We plowed forward with various new ideas, and as do all gardeners, we had our successes and our failures.

To offset the vagaries of rainfall, we used an irrigation system to help water our garden. Nearby Beaver Creek gave us a steady source of water. Dad provided the equipment and know-how, and my brother and I worked hard getting the water to our plants.

One particularly dry period in late May, we watered a lot. After about two weeks we noted that our plants were discolored

and stunted. Our years of gardening experience told us that
something was wrong. We racked our brains to determine the
problem. Had we skimped on the fertilizer? No, we had spread
the normal amount of cow manure. Was it a late year? No, the
temperature had been normal, so this could not account for the
discoloration and stunting. Had we misused an insecticide or
herbicide? No, we had not applied any herbicide, and though we
had applied insecticides, they were the same ones we had been
using for years. Moreover, our insecticide use would not account
for these symptoms.

We never proved what had ruined our garden, but we had
one major suspect: the irrigation water. We had relied exten-
sively on irrigation water from Beaver Creek during the drought.
We never tested the water, but we knew that a golf course lay
upstream. In addition, grapes and other crops were grown next
to the stream. In the 1960s few controls regulated the use of her-
bicides. With hindsight, we are quite certain that the creek wa-
ter was contaminated with just enough herbicides to stunt our
plants, but not enough to kill them. Our garden survived, but the
harvest fell short of expectations.

America is a country of survivors. My family survived a ruined garden, our
country survived the terrorist attacks of 9/11, and we are all managing to
carry on despite the widespread pollution of our waters. Nevertheless,
frustrated with their inability to use nuisance law or the Clean Water Act
to remedy pollution from AFOs and other agricultural activities, the public may seek alternative options. Lawsuits and regulations dealing with
dangerous pesticides suggest two directions. First, legal principles underlying liability for water contamination by pesticides may be used to hold
agricultural producers accountable for nutrient pollution. Second, states
may adopt regulatory management practices from pesticide-collection
programs as responses to contamination problems.

Contamination of Water

Agricultural activities including AFOs, the use of pesticides and fertilizers,
and certain cultivation practices are causing egregious pollution. Many
fields near CAFOs contain too much nitrogen and phosphorus, which
then drain into water sources. Scientists have found more than sixty pes-

ticides in groundwater in thirty states.[1] Most of these pesticides come from agriculture. Tons of soil are deposited in streams and rivers each spring after fields are plowed. With such water contamination facing us, what are we doing? Is our government taking appropriate action to contain the problem and rectify existing contaminated waters? How are we assigning blame and liability for this contamination? These and other questions remain to be answered. Governmental bodies have taken action, but some members of the public have judged current regulations to be insufficient.

Lackadaisical governmental responses to water contamination and risks posed by pesticides such as the chemical Alar have left the public apprehensive. Indeed, many Americans doubt our government's ability to protect us against carcinogens. The pollution discovered at Love Canal (1978) and the water contamination highlighted by the book and movie *A Civil Action* (1998) and the movie *Erin Brockovich* (2000) show that governmental regulation of harmful chemicals has been inadequate.

Farmers have additional worries about water contamination. They depend on groundwater for their drinking water, and their animals often rely on water sources on the farm. In addition, public outcry over a health concern can affect their operations. The sharp drop in apple prices during the Alar incident shows that consumers can disrupt an established market and cause major financial problems for farmers if they feel that governmental regulations are inadequate. In fact, some states felt a need to respond with agricultural-product-disparagement laws, whereby producers of perishable food products can sue persons who disseminate false statements about the safety of their products.[2]

More recent federal restrictions on pesticides, federal conservation-compliance provisions, and sustainable-agriculture initiatives acknowledge legislative interest in responding to the public's concern about safety. Public attitudes are leading to additional monitoring of food and water supplies and proposals for more comprehensive safety legislation. These will affect agricultural production. Farmers need to be ready to adjust to new requirements, proscriptions, and markets as legislatures respond to public concerns about health and safety issues.

Pesticides—including insecticides, herbicides, and fungicides—are a major source of contamination. Each year we use about 600 million pounds of pesticides in the United States.[3] Herbicides—to control weeds—account for 70 percent of the pesticides used.[4] Five major crops—corn, cotton, soybeans, wheat, and fall potatoes—account for 86 percent of our agricultural herbicide use and 54 percent of insecticide use.[5] Our country's corn crop, by far occupying the largest acreage of any crop, receives about

43 percent of the pesticides.[6] Of the major crops, rice is the most intensive user of herbicides on a per-acre basis.[7]

Not everything about pesticides is gloomy, however. Our use of pesticides has been decreasing since 1982, mainly because farmers are planting less acreage.[8] Integrated pest-management practices can help reduce the use of pesticides as well, and scientists project that improvements in weed management will decrease the need for herbicides on some crops.[9] At the same time, the pesticides still in use are safer—less toxic and less harmful to the environment—than the pesticides used a generation ago, for health and safety concerns have led us to remove some of the more dangerous pesticides from the market.

Liability for Water Contamination

Persons injured by agricultural nutrients, including those from CAFOs, have several legal arguments for securing redress. The most obvious is to show a violation of a law. I will term such an infraction a "violation of regulation." Other legal bases for relief include strict liability, negligence, nuisance, and trespass. Liability under these arguments varies from state to state, but analyses of them illustrate issues important in the development of policy recommendations for addressing damages from nutrient contamination.

Past lawsuits can show us how plaintiffs have used these arguments to hold persons liable for injuries they cause. A majority of the cases involve pesticides, but the lessons of pesticide contamination are pertinent to injuries from water contamination by agricultural nutrients.

Violation of a Regulation

Persons producing, handling, and using nutrients can incur liability if they violate a regulation or statute. The term *regulation* is used here to include laws (statutes) enacted by legislative bodies and rules adopted by administrative agencies. Safety regulations, regulations establishing standards, and permit regulations are common types of environmental regulations that create liability. The expansion of federal and state regulations for agricultural activities increases the potential for lawsuits based on violation of a regulation.

Violations of safety regulations or regulations establishing standards ordinarily are outright negligence (negligence per se) if the regulation expresses a policy for the protection of a certain class of persons. An injured person need not show negligence in such cases; it exists because the regulation was violated. Both the harm and the injured party, however, must fall into classes specifically covered by the regulation. Moreover, even if a plaintiff establishes negligence under a regulation, various defenses can absolve the defendant from liability. Common-law and statutory defenses of assumption of risk, contributory negligence, and proximate cause can defeat liability.

Many states are adopting regulations requiring persons to apply manure and fertilizer according to soil- and nutrient-management plans. In those states failure to apply manure as required constitutes negligence per se. If injured persons can prove that the applicator's deviation from the management plan caused injuries, the applicator could incur liability. If the deviation led to the contamination of water, the applicator would be liable for damages from this contamination as well.

A court considering injuries from the use of a pesticide inconsistent with its label adopted the negligence per se rationale.[10] The court decided that the statutory labeling law modified common law. As a safety statute, the labeling law sought to prevent harm from the improper use of dangerous pesticides to people, animals, and plants. Any deviation from the label was negligence per se. Anyone failing to follow label instructions and harming another by the resulting contamination should be held accountable.

Not all safety, standards, and permitting regulations trigger negligence per se to ease the burden of proof for injured persons. Even regulations that appear similar can differ significantly. Some safety regulations are general in scope and require that a plaintiff prove negligence. For example, a Texas court considered an action for damages from water contamination in which the pollution violated a safety rule.[11] The court noted that although some rules impose negligence per se, some do not. Analyzing the Texas rules protecting freshwater, the court found that liability required a specific finding of negligence.

Alternatively, a violation of regulation may involve failure to secure a permit for a CAFO,[12] and the law or regulation may assign penalties for not having a permit. Violation of a permit regulation therefore provides a legal argument under which we can assess penalties. If a permit regulation delineates substantive standards and failure to secure a permit leads to harm of a type covered by the regulation, failure to secure a permit generally is negligence. In such cases, however, plaintiffs must usually prove the negligence.

Strict Liability

Under statutory or common law, a court can hold that farmers contaminating water by using dangerous substances such as pesticides are absolutely liable for damages under a strict-liability standard. In such cases plaintiffs need not prove negligence. Strict liability also reduces the defenses available to defeat an action for damages. Given that disposal of manure or animal waste and other agricultural activities are not abnormally dangerous, strict liability would not be an appropriate cause of action for most types of agricultural pollution.

Negligence

To show liability based on negligence for water contamination by nutrients, a plaintiff must prove the existence of a duty, a breach of a duty of care, causation, and damages. In most situations this will require evidence both that the polluter knew or should have known that his or her activity would be likely to cause the injury and that the activity caused the injury. The difficult burden of establishing proof for this theory means that plaintiffs will prefer to establish legal arguments in strict liability, private nuisance, or violation of regulation.

However, liability under negligence is significant after evidence of contamination becomes known, since tardy remedial response to contamination may lead to liability. If a farmer continues to dispose of manure in a manner known to cause contamination, the farmer can be considered negligent and subjected to liability for the resulting injuries and damages.

In addition, negligent conduct of an extraordinary nature involving actual or implied malice can justify awards of punitive damages. A polluter who fails to reveal the existence of the pollution to neighboring properties may be liable for punitive damages.[13] A polluter who acts with wanton or reckless disregard for the rights of others, such as disregarding the serious risks of groundwater contamination, may be forced to pay punitive damages.

Nuisances

Most farmers know both how nuisance law can restrict agricultural operations and how right-to-farm laws can protect them. In the context of the release of nutrients from an AFO, an injury from substantial and unreasonable interference with the use and enjoyment of property could lead to liability as a private nuisance. Actions in private nuisance are possible when the interference is accidental and otherwise actionable under rules controlling liability for negligent conduct. Liability in nuisance is predicated on unreasonable injury rather than on unreasonable conduct. Past cases show that contamination of water can constitute an actionable nuisance.[14]

Trespass

If a farmer allows nutrients from his operations to invade the property of another, a plaintiff may claim trespass. Trespass can be similar to a nuisance, with a single activity being both a nuisance and a trespass. A nuisance involves an interference with another's enjoyment of property, however, while a trespass generally involves an intrusion onto the property. Both approaches raise the question of intent: is intent required, or can we impose liability for unintentional trespass? Generally, unintentional entries accompanied by negligence can be found to constitute trespass.

Lawsuits confirm that a surface invasion of polluted water is a trespass. If a farmer pollutes a stream and harms a downstream landowner, there is a trespass and the farmer is liable for damages. Trespass can involve excessive pollution of surface water from a commercial feedlot where injuries are shown.[15]

Liability for subsurface invasions presents a more debatable issue. Some legal authorities argue that we should not appraise subsurface invasions of liquids as a trespass both because the invasion is indirect rather than direct and because the invasion is actionable under nuisance law. The abandonment of distinction between direct and indirect invasions, however, and other modifications of the law suggest that underground contamination of water will likely be found to constitute an actionable trespass in some states. Knowledge that water or harmful nutrients are seeping into a neighboring property may support a finding of a trespass.[16]

Managing Unwanted Pesticides

With respect to water contamination, AFOs cannot be separated from other agricultural sources of contamination, such as pesticides. To safeguard public health and prevent contamination, however, pesticides have already been subjected to an exacting set of federal and state regulations, which include procedures for removing pesticides from the market if they harm the environment unacceptably. Moreover, impressive scientific efforts have led to integrated pesticide-management programs that reduce the use of pesticides.

Indeed, farmers are often reluctant to dispose of unwanted pesticides for fear of doing something illegal. Moreover, convenient methods for safely disposing of pesticides are often not readily available. Survey results from Iowa,[17] Minnesota,[18] and Vermont[19] suggest that the lack of viable disposal options leads most persons with quantities of unwanted pesticides to continue to store them. In addition, farmers usually are unwilling to incur the full cost of legal disposal. Without government intervention, therefore, unwanted pesticides are likely to be left in their current storage locations. Some, however, end up buried on a farm, dumped in a landfill, or dispersed into the environment, where they can cause a pollution problem. Since such disposal methods are not environmentally sound—and since estimates blame unwanted chemicals for hundreds of deaths and thousands of illnesses yearly in our country—governments have decided to intervene.

The significant quantities of unwanted pesticides stored in barns and other outbuildings throughout the country can lead to environmental contamination, especially in a natural disaster. A tornado or a flood can disperse stored pesticides into the ground or water. In addition, when farm properties are sold or inherited, pesticides may be passed to persons with no training or experience in using or disposing of them safely. Governments at all levels have expressed an interest in dealing with problems such as these.

To address these stocks of pesticides, states have developed agricultural-pesticide collection programs, typically voluntary programs for persons who want to dispose of unwanted pesticides. These regulatory provisions offer ideas for developing long-term programs for reducing other kinds of environmental risks as well. The organization and funding provisions may be particularly significant for developing responses to pollution from AFOs.

An Unwanted-Pesticide Problem

A steady stream of new pesticides has become available since the 1950s. New information on older pesticides has often revealed that they are unsafe, leading to their withdrawal from the marketplace. The Federal Insecticide, Fungicide, and Rodenticide Act, administered by the EPA, addresses the most obvious problems involving canceled and suspended pesticides. However, farmers may have relatively small quantities of canceled pesticides they did not return for indemnification. In addition, farmers often switch to new, more effective pesticides, leaving them with registered pesticides they no longer use. In other situations, new production practices have led farmers to hire contractors for pesticide applications, so that the farmers' stocks of pesticides remain unused. Canceled and unused pesticides, jointly called "unwanted" pesticides, create a disposal problem. In the early 1990s experts estimated that there were 13 million pounds of unwanted pesticides in the Great Lakes basin.[20]

Given that farmers are the main users of pesticides, they pose the greatest danger in misusing pesticides or treating unwanted pesticides in ways that create unnecessary risks of accidents or contamination. All states have adopted legislation regulating conduct involving the use of pesticides that can harm humans or the environment. The legislation provides civil and criminal penalties for the misuse of pesticides but not for the improper storage of unwanted pesticides. Future misuse, spills, and acts of God can cause major harm or environmental damage, however—risks we can eliminate via the safe disposal of unwanted pesticides.

Governmental Oversight

States have recognized the problems that farmers' unwanted pesticides create. In response to dangers arising from the improper disposal of canceled, suspended, and unused agricultural pesticides—and from the storage of unwanted agricultural pesticides—forty-seven states have implemented some type of pesticide collection program.[21] These programs involve voluntary participation by persons wanting to dispose of unwanted pesticides. A 1996 survey found that nearly 10 million pounds of pesticides have been collected under these programs.[22]

Pesticide collection efforts vary considerably from state to state, and programs in a number of states have changed over time. Some states combine pesticides with other hazardous materials under a single collection program. All pesticide collection programs operate within the federal legal framework addressing hazardous-waste management that provides for human and environmental safety. For unwanted pesticides that are hazardous waste, the Universal Waste Rule applies to state pesticide collection programs.[23] Anyone (including farmers) taking pesticides to a collection program need not meet the paperwork normally required to dispose of hazardous waste. Persons managing agricultural pesticides in conjunction with a collection program qualify as handlers of universal wastes. Under the handler provisions, we do not require the normal manifest procedure for dealing with hazardous wastes.

Safety and Liability Concerns

Weighty concerns about safety and liability accompanied states' initial forays into the collection of unwanted pesticides. These considerations prompted some states to schedule site visits before beginning the collection program. Early collection programs also included on-site pickups, but the expense involved led to central collection sites. Although mishaps may occur when participants bring unwanted pesticides to a central collection site, as happens under household hazardous-waste programs, most states have found the risk to be acceptable and have discontinued on-site pickups except in special situations. Moreover, despite an occasional contained spill, these programs have excellent safety records.

In most cases states officially sanction collection sites. For programs without permanent sites, commercial enterprises and county highway garages have volunteered their facilities as collection sites. Such sites often have a paved area, running water, electricity, sanitary facilities, and garbage disposal. Regulations enabling governmental officials to obtain samples of unidentified pesticides before the owners bring them to the collection site allow these materials to be handled in a safe manner. Regulations and bid specifications make the hazardous-waste contractor responsible for furnishing all other materials, equipment, and services to collect the pesticides safely. Containers may be offered to participants requesting assistance for damaged or leaking containers. Toll-free telephone numbers for emergencies or problems with transportation constitute another safety feature.

Registration and Appointments

Many state agricultural-pesticide collection programs include registration procedures. Agency personnel distribute forms to potential participants, and farmers can register if they have unwanted pesticides they wish to dispose of safely. Registration generally provides information on the condition of pesticide containers and the location and type of material to be collected. The registration procedure lets the state secure information on the types and amounts of pesticides that farmers want to have collected. This information can be used to decide what should be collected given available financial resources. Registration also provides information for the development of bid specifications and facilitates the arrangement of special collection efforts where needed.

Other benefits often accompany a registration program. Farmers examining stored pesticides sometimes discover useful products. In addition, they can discover problems with the condition of pesticide containers. Registration information also facilitates scheduling specific times for collection, thus alleviating traffic congestion at the collection site, avoiding long waiting periods for participants, and reducing the risk of a mishap.

The need for registration abates as accumulations of unwanted pesticides are collected or as a state gains experience in managing a collection program. Abandoning registration makes participating easier. Iowa registers applicants by phone, thus reducing the administrative work involved in its collection program. Persons with unwanted pesticides and other wastes can book an appointment within two weeks of the delivery of their materials. While making an appointment, people can also ask staffers questions about the disposal of other wastes, such as paint, used motor oil, and batteries. Agency personnel meet participants at the collection site to confirm the scheduled appointment and to direct them to the appropriate locations at the site.

Funding Collection Programs

Funding availability is the major constraint on pesticide-collection efforts. The lawful disposal of unwanted pesticides is expensive. Many persons have stored unwanted pesticides because they are unwilling to pay for disposal. This expense affects state governments's pesticide-collection programs, too. Costs for early pesticide collection programs in the Great Lakes basin were approximately four dollars per pound.[24]

Although states fund pesticide-collections through existing environmental programs, they also generate funds specifically for the collection programs using the following four methods, either alone or in combination: (1) grants, (2) user fees, (3) state pesticide-registration fees, and (4) taxes on the sale of pesticides. Each state can thus adopt a strategy that corresponds to its resources and political situation.

Federal and state funding has covered some collection-program costs. Grants for pesticide-collections have come from the EPA pursuant to various federal programs or special state appropriations. Reliance solely on this form of financing, however, is not conducive to a long-term program, as governmental programs may end.

Some states charge user fees, but most do not because they discourage participation. For example, 57 percent of over 1,000 Georgia farmers responding to a survey stated they would not be willing to pay for the disposal of their unwanted pesticides.[25] Minnesota adopted regulations incorporating user fees only after a threshold, so that 95 percent of the participants did not incur a fee.[26] In any event, user fees involve an inordinate amount of effort to raise insignificant sums. Since user fees often do not cover the costs of disposal, states need other sources of funds.

Registration fees or taxes may constitute a major source of funds for collection programs in some states. Using registration fees in this way involves enacting a law or an administrative regulation that assesses a fee on the yearly registration of each pesticide and the identification of part of the fee for collection and environmental programs. Alternatively, a tax on pesticide products, such as adopted in Michigan, can help fund pesticide-collection programs. Using registration fees and product taxes to fund collection programs ties pesticide costs to disposal costs.

Encouraging Environmental Stewardship

This overview of liability and management responses for pesticide contamination suggests opportunities for developing responses for nutrient pollution from agriculture. With the advent of permitting, licensing, certification, and nutrient-management provisions for AFOs, governments have gained methods to address environmental problems. If governments decline to act, individual citizens can resort to liability causes of action. The improper use of pesticides reveals two major causes of action to use against persons causing nutrient pollution or other problems. Lawsuits grounded on common-law actions of negligence and trespass can provide relief. In suits based on negligence, a farmer's violation of a regulation would be evidence of negligence that lends support to the private cause of action.

Deliberations over pesticides show that new regulations can address dangers inherent in activities. While contaminants from AFOs are not as serious as contaminants from pesticides, governments may respond to anticipated nutrient problems that accompany AFOs through new programs. Experiences with pesticide-collection programs show that multiple collections over a number of years were necessary to remove most accumulated stocks. Moreover, states drew on existing regulatory expertise, such as the Cooperative Extension Service, to increase participation. These lessons may be applied to AFOs. Americans should not expect a "quick fix" under new regulations. It will take time to address the pollution issues from AFOs, and governments might want to work through existing channels to assist operators in structuring their operations to eliminate objectionable pollutants.

Costs are an important consideration in addressing environmental problems. Once states gained experience and removed large quantities of stored pesticides, they could forgo some practices and move to less costly programs. The collection of unwanted pesticides also showed that producers needed financial incentives—the free disposal of their unwanted pesticides—to encourage participation. If we decide to help address environmental problems accompanying AFOs, funds will be needed. Agencies can be expected to need more resources to monitor and enforce existing provisions. States might contemplate how they can obtain the financial resources both to help those who need it and to enforce environmental regulations.

At the same time, we might encourage additional governmental efforts to ascribe pollutants' costs to animal production and provide incentives for abating pollution. One possibility is a regulatory structure that incorporates a "polluter-pays" principle. Registration fees and taxes on animal products could relate environmental costs to animal production. Fees and taxes on waste products and fertilizers could provide incentives to engage in acceptable management practices. Alternatively, users of water might be taxed to provide money to be used in tempering pollution. Nutrient contamination calls for a continuing source of funds to provide a permanent solution.

NOTES

1. Sandra Batie, W. E. Cox, and P. L. Diebel, *Managing Agricultural Contamination of Groundwater: State Strategies* (Washington, D.C.: National Governors' Association, 1989).

2. J. Brent Hagy, "Comment: Let Them Eat Beef: The Constitutionality of the Texas False Disparagement of Perishable Food Products Act," *Texas Tech Law Review* 29 (1998): 851–84.

3. U.S. Department of Agriculture, Economic Research Service, *Pesticide Management in U.S. Agriculture* (Washington, D.C.: USDA, 1999).

4. Biing-Hwan Lin, M. Padgitt, L. Bull, H. Delvo, D. Shank, and H. Taylor, *Pesticide and Fertilizer Use and Trends in U.S. Agriculture,* Agricultural Economic Report, no. 717 (Washington, D.C.: USDA, Economic Research Service, 1995), 31.

5. Ibid., 10.

6. Ibid., 4.

7. Ibid., 32.

8. Ibid., 31.

9. Jorge Fernandez-Cornejo and Sharon Jans, *Pest Management in U.S. Agriculture,* Economic Research Service Report, Agricultural Handbook, no. 717 (Washington, D.C.: USDA, Economic Research Service, 1999), 25.

10. Bennett v. Larsen Company, 540 N.W.2d 540 (Wis. 1984).

11. Murfee v. Phillips Petroleum Company, 492 S.W.2d 667 (Tex Civ. App. 1973).

12. Water Keeper Alliance, Inc. v. Smithfield Foods, Inc., 53 ERC (BNA) 1506; 32 ELR 20320 (2001).

13. Exxon Corp. v. Yarema, 516 A.2d 990, 1005 (Md. 1986).

14. Ibid.

15. Atkinson v. Herington Cattle Co., 436 P.2d 816 (Kansas 1968).

16. Furrer v. Talent Irrigation District, 466 P.2d 605, 615 (Or. 1970).

17. R. D. DeWitt, *Household Hazardous Materials Toxic Cleanup Days* (Des Moines: Iowa Department of Natural Resources, 1997), vi.

18. Joseph Spitzmueller, *1994 Report of Waste Pesticide Collection in Minnesota* (St. Paul: Minnesota Department of Agriculture, 1995), 33.

19. Allen Karnatz, *Obsolete Pesticide Disposal Project* (Montpelier: Vermont Department of Agriculture, Food, and Markets, 1991), 18.

20. Margaret Jones, *Agricultural Clean Sweep: Waste Pesticide Removals 1988–1992* (Chicago: EPA, region 5, 1993), 2.

21. C. P. Cubbage, *State Agricultural Pesticide Collections Survey* (Lansing: Michigan Department of Agriculture, 1996), 1–23.

22. Ibid.

23. *Code of Federal Regulations,* title 40, pt. 273.

24. Jones, *Agricultural Clean Sweep,* 3.

25. Tolar, *Survey Summary: Georgia 1997 Farm Chemical Survey* (Atlanta: Georgia Department of Agriculture, 1997).

26. Spitzmueller, *1994 Report,* 29.

10 Accountability and Enforcement

*O*ur farm was not far from a city. People who lived there often went for drives in the countryside, which they also used for hunting and fishing. To the northwest lay the major railroad connecting Buffalo (and the Northeast) to Cleveland (and the Midwest), paralleled by a service road that was open and accessible to vehicles. Hunters, hikers, and others used this service road for quick access to the overgrown fields and woods that bordered our farm.

During my youth we did not have to worry about hunters—there were no wild animals worth hunting, except occasional migratory Canada geese and ducks. In the late 1960s, however, the farmland owned by our neighbor west of our hayfields became overgrown with brush and small trees. Native deer and wild turkey populations became reestablished. Desirable game fish, muskrats, and weasels reappeared in the creeks. Gradually, hunters, anglers, and trappers became more prevalent.

Our farm was completely fenced: it was a necessity with dairy animals. Yet hunters would ignore these fences and come on our

*farm in search of their prey. We were concerned that they not mis-
take a cow for a deer, of course, but fortunately no hunter made
this mistake.*

The family dog was not so lucky.

*It was in mid-November, and Dad was out in the vineyard. He
had started his winter's work of pruning each grape vine. As he
slowly moved from vine to vine, our dog scouted the surrounding
area. She loved to chase rabbits, raccoons, or whatever animal
happened to be around. Then Dad heard her barking. This was
not unusual. She would do this when she had chased a rabbit into
a hole or had treed a raccoon. Suddenly there was a shotgun blast,
followed by silence—the barking had ceased.*

*Dad hastened toward the scene. He saw a hunter with a gun
standing near our dead dog. When the hunter saw Dad, he started
running northwest to the railroad. Dad yelled, but the hunter kept
running. Given the situation—a defenseless farmer facing an
armed hunter—Dad returned to the house. After telling Mom
what had happened, he took a shovel and buried the dog to spare
the rest of the family from the gruesome sight.*

Like my dad, many of us feel helpless in addressing wrongs. Despite all our
laws and regulations, and the various agencies for enforcing them, wrongs
sometimes go unpunished. In some situations the perpetrators know they
have violated a law. In other cases persons may honestly believe that their
conduct was legitimate. Of course, we cannot expect our government to
address every possible wrong, but we strive to create a workable democracy that is open and fair.

Taking Action against Polluters

Numerous laws and regulations have been enacted to prevent all sorts of
pollution from harming people and degrading the environment. But do
our governmental activities address the conduct underlying the problems? Do the enforcement mechanisms lead to the prosecution and punishment of violators? Answering these questions will help tell us whether
polluters are held accountable for their transgressions and whether our
governments are effectively reducing offensive pollution.

The first question involves accountability, while the second involves
enforcement. To apportion accountability, governments must first iden-

tify pollution problems and select regulatory responses. If a regulation does not confront the problem, or we have misdiagnosed the problem, we won't achieve the environmental quality we want. Once regulations are in place, potential violators must learn their responsibilities and become aware of deterrence and restitution measures. To deter potential polluters, moreover, the penalties must be harsh enough to encourage persons to cease objectionable activities.

Reasonable regulatory controls alone, however, cannot control pollution. The second question thus asks whether we are enforcing the regulations. Enforcement provisions must designate responsibilities and assign them to regulators. In addition, those regulators will require resources and personnel, as well as the willingness to enforce regulations. If violators are not concerned about being prosecuted, they have little incentive to obey regulatory proscriptions and may continue to discharge illegal pollutants into the environment.

Public information regarding spills from lagoons, fish kills, and other pollution events demonstrates that AFOs have a pollution problem. The Natural Resources Defense Council estimates that there were more than 1,000 spills or pollution incidents at livestock facilities in ten states during a four-year period in the late 1990s.[1] To avoid perpetuating such an unacceptable situation, we must identify the causes of these events. How many were due to poor management, how many were due to bad practices (such as siting a lagoon in a floodplain), and how many were violations of the law? For pollution events that did not involve the violation of a law, we may want to enact additional regulations. For those that did, we need to learn why they occurred. Are producers violating laws because they are not concerned about the possibility of a penalty? Were the pollution incidents mishaps that probably will not occur again? Answers to these questions can help us develop better responses to unacceptable pollution events.

Accountability of AFO Regulations

The initial issue is whether current laws and regulations respond to the pollution generated by AFOs.[2] Both federal and state laws are important: the federal government's National Pollutant Discharge Elimination System (NPDES) permit requirements of the Clean Water Act apply to CAFOs, and our states have established their own distinct requirements that help reduce contamination from AFOs—including CAFOs. Finally, those AFOs not covered in these first two categories are subject to federal and state non-point-source pollution provisions. Therefore, to examine accountability, we can differentiate three groups of AFOs: (1) those regulated as CAFOs under federal law, (2) those subject to state AFO laws, and (3) those that are not regulated by point-source or state AFO regulations. The possibility exists that operations in at least one of these categories are adequately regulated, while those in another are creating offensive pollution.

Federal Law for Point Sources

Federal law specifies conditions under which persons contaminating water from point sources are subject to penalties. CAFOs are subject to these regulations. Point-source pollution provisions are violated whenever a CAFO fails to secure an NPDES permit.[3] The possession of a permit, however, does not ensure compliance. Any noncompliance with the permit's requirements is a violation of federal law as well.

Determining compliance may present difficulties. In a case involving an enforcement action by the attorney general of Iowa, the owner of a hog-confinement operation contended that the state did not prove pollution of state waters.[4] The tenacious owner argued against the civil penalties all the way to the Iowa Supreme Court. The court found that the evidence, including surface pollution and a putrid discharge from excessive concentrations of manure, was sufficient to uphold civil fines of $59,000.

More fundamentally, we may ask whether our federal law even addresses the situations that result in a polluting event. Federal regulations define CAFOs partly in terms of the number of animals at the facility. Such criteria overlook the possibility of pollution problems associated with concentrations of AFOs in an area. Two moderate-sized AFOs next to each other may together generate excess nutrients that need to be regulated. This suggests that the criterion of animal numbers per facility may not be adequate in responding to potential pollution problems.

The federal regulations also regulate AFOs based on ten-year, twenty-five-year, and one-hundred-year storm events.[5] Here again, it may be inappropriate to apply the same standards to all AFOs. Larger AFOs and areas with several AFOs have larger spills and leaks, which would cause greater damages.[6] Rainfall standards should perhaps be more exacting for these facilities.

Does ignorance of permit requirements or an accidental release of prohibited contaminants lead to fines or other civil liability under federal law? As with other laws, ignorance, mistakes, and accidents are not excused. Violations of federal point-source pollution regulations produce liability despite the violator's lack of knowledge or intent. Although an operator may employ good-faith efforts to comply with the law, such efforts are not a defense against liability, although they may be considered in assessing the amount of a civil penalty. Of course, exceptions exist for emergencies: federal CAFO regulations provide that discharges may occur due to upset and bypass events.

State AFO Regulations

Most states have recently adopted or amended provisions specifically aimed at regulating some AFOs. The regulations delineate nutrient- and manure-management requirements to counter nutrient contamination. These regulations begin with licensing and certification provisions for persons operating livestock facilities or preparing nutrient-management plans. State provisions regulate lagoons through odor, design, and inspection requirements as well. Some states require guarantees for the closure of facilities. The novelty and variety of state provisions make it difficult to determine whether they meaningfully address pollution discharged from AFOs.

It is not clear whether state regulations are deterring polluters. Concomitantly, it is unclear whether some states have the means to enforce their regulations meaningfully. When enforcing AFO provisions, state agencies use procedures established with respect to other pollution regulations. Such procedures normally commence with an oral warning, a warning letter, a notice of discharge, or a notice of violation. A warning notice identifies transgressions and indicates the regulatory provision being violated. The notice informs the violator of the unacceptable condition and specifies a time period during which the problem must be fixed. Warnings give persons an opportunity to correct the problem without facing a fine or other sanction.

Once notified, an alleged violator who fails to remedy the identified problem within the prescribed time frame can be fined. In some cases state AFO provisions prescribe the fine. In other cases states use the penalty provisions set forth for environmental violations. If an agency feels a fine is not a sufficient penalty, it can seek a cease-and-desist order to force compliance. The state can use such a court order to force an AFO operator to discontinue a polluting activity or stop raising animals.

Detection of violations raises a more challenging problem. How does a state agency learn of a violation, and how does the state prove the violation? For example, many state AFO regulations prohibit the overapplication of manure to land that results in the contamination of waters. But how do governmental agencies monitor compliance? Rather obviously, a state will have difficulty in establishing proof that a particular over-application of manure is responsible for a water-quality violation.

Complexities in monitoring compliance explain why governments attempt to induce AFO operators to adopt voluntary management measures to reduce the potential for contamination. Overseeing an enforcement program is often too time-consuming. Disbursing funds and resources to encourage widespread acceptance of best management practices may do more to reduce contamination by AFOs than would taking the same resources and applying them to enforcement programs.

Two related issues suggest caution in assessing state AFO regulations. First, we might want to compare the seriousness of pollution from AFOs to that of pollutants from other sources. States where other polluters present problems more severe than those created by AFOs may well direct their efforts and resources to the former. Second, the lack of enforcement of existing regulations can mean that the best environmental regulations will fail to achieve their objectives. Experience suggests that vigilance is needed to keep a state agency on track in its enforcement responsibilities.

AFOs Not Regulated by Point-Source or State AFO Regulations

While the accountability provisions of numerous federal and state regulations lay the groundwork to reduce contamination from those AFOs subject to the regulations, thousands of other AFOs fall outside these requirements. The federal requirements apply only to CAFOs. Not all states have specialized AFO regulations, and many regulate only large operations. This means that most AFOs are subject only to federal and state non-point-source pollution requirements. Do current non-point-source pollution provisions adequately address contamination problems that emanate from these otherwise unregulated AFOs?

Generally, provisions governing non-point-source pollution recommend voluntary practices to minimize an activity's potentially adverse effects. We know these as best management practices, which are simply methods, measures, and practices available to reduce or eliminate waterborne pollutants. Lagoons, storage structures, riparian buffers, filter strips, fencing, crop rotation, and nutrient-management plans are tactics for intercepting non-point-source pollutants from AFOs.

State and federal responses to non-point-source pollution also involve financial and technical assistance. Regulators have used a range of planning, technical assistance, cost-sharing, and public-funding initiatives to help with controlling non-point-source pollution. Although such positive regulations should be encouraged, they do not proscribe pollution.

This leaves other non-point-source pollution regulations as the only avenue for addressing this type of pollution. Every state has general authority to deal with non-point-source discharges under the powers reserved to it by the Constitution. Two groups of regulation are prevalent: (1) general restrictions of non-point-source discharge enacted through permits and (2) prohibitions of non-point-source pollution. The first group consists of state laws containing general discharge prohibitions under which a permit for enumerated discharges is required. These provisions can set up a non-point-source permitting program and specify remedial responses to discharges. Some of these general provisions incorporate exceptions for agriculture that lessen the scope of their coverage.

The second group involves prohibitions against non-point-source pollution. These laws simply bar enumerated activities known to harm water quality unacceptably, which requires linking the discharge to the condition of the water. Proving such violations can be difficult.

Whatever their authority in this sphere, most state agencies are not holding non-point-source polluters accountable for their infractions. Enforcing the relevant laws presents formidable challenges. How do regulatory agencies find the violation? Once they learn of an alleged violation, how do they prove that the activity violates the law? Moreover, penalties are not a prominent component of non-point-source pollution provisions.

Given these circumstances, we must conclude that AFOs not regulated by federal CAFO or state AFO regulations are not subject to meaningful accountability provisions. These AFOs can engage in polluting activities because they are not concerned about penalties. The numbers of AFOs in this category vary from state to state. Maryland[7] and Minnesota[8] regulate most AFOs, so few animal operations there fall into this category. In other states, most AFOs may remain outside meaningful regulation.

Discharging Enforcement Responsibilities

Environmental enforcement involves designating an agency or official to enforce the law. For water pollution from AFOs, the enforcer is designated pursuant to the cooperative federalism provisions of the Clean Water Act. This typically means a state's environmental agency is in charge of enforcing water-pollution provisions.

With a regulator in place, we can move to the twin issues of resources and personnel. Has the government provided sufficient financial resources for meaningful enforcement? Next, does the agency have a commitment to enforce? All too often political issues incline agencies to forgo effective enforcement. In part because of this, we may ask another question: do lawsuits by citizens constitute an appropriate mechanism for responding to environmental problems caused by CAFOs?

We often cannot tell whether an enforcement agency is unwilling to enforce the law or simply lacks the personnel to do so. Whatever the cause, egregious pollution from many CAFOs demonstrates that enforcement responsibilities are not being discharged. Facing unregulated industrial hog operations in Indiana, citizens sought to compel the EPA to assume enforcement of NPDES permits there.[9] In 2001 the EPA established a deadline for the state of Michigan to comply with federal CAFO regulations, culminating in an agreement in January 2002 for protecting water quality from manure runoff.[10]

Environmental groups such as the Sierra Club[11] and Waterkeeper Alliance[12] have taken it on themselves to assist enforcers by filing citizen suits. These cases suggest a breakdown in enforcement responsibilities, with scant governmental oversight of CAFOs and their deleterious activities. Moreover, if governments are failing to enforce CAFO regulations, we may assume that even less enforcement occurs with respect to environmental impairment from AFOs.

Designating an Enforcer

Under many environmental statutes, federal agencies commission states to enforce federal laws. They authorize this through an agreement known as a "memorandum of agreement" or a "memorandum of understanding." For laws managed by the EPA, a state and an EPA regional office execute an annual agreement setting forth enforcement commitments.[13]

Although federal agencies generally retain enforcement authority, and can reclaim this authority from a state, limited resources and difficulties in monitoring compliance make federal enforcement rare. The EPA has authorized forty-five states to administer NPDES permits[14] and, concomitantly, to enforce federal CAFO regulations. State governments are enforcing a majority of our water-pollution regulations.

Because enforcement occurs at the state level, the proficiency and rigor of enforcement efforts display considerable variation. A state whose population supports environmental quality may elect to place more resources and greater emphasis on enforcement matters. States with large populations may have more specialized staffs with greater expertise than do less populous ones, which thus tend to be less effective in enforcing environmental regulations. Counties and municipalities that handle enforcement at the local level can suffer from this same inadequacy.

A government lacking the expertise or resources to enforce its laws adequately may look to the delegating government to handle enforcement matters. A county may look to the state; the state, to the EPA regional office. Yet most delegating governments do not allocate funds for the enforcement measures it has assigned to other governments. Therefore, governments lacking expertise or funding will not have a meaningful enforcement program.

Commencing an Action

Willingness and diligence in conducting enforcement measures constitute another variable. Depending on circumstances, placing enforcement authority at a lower or higher level of government can enhance or detract the likelihood of prosecuting violators. Sometimes state and local governments have greater sensitivity to local public criticism than does a federal agency. In these cases the lower government may prosecute environmental violations more diligently. Nevertheless, local and even state governments can be reluctant to prosecute individuals or firms that are well connected politically or important to an area's economy. Taking action against a neighbor may be difficult as well. In these cases a higher level of government may be more effective in commencing appropriate enforcement actions.

Enforcement mechanisms involve warnings, civil penalties, injunctive relief, and criminal prosecutions. At the federal level lawyers for agencies in charge of environmental issues most often handle administrative enforcement matters. The Department of Justice generally handles enforcement measures involving prosecution, however, which restricts the environmental agency's ability to set enforcement priorities and decide how rigorously to enforce selected provisions. The timing of enforcement can also be an issue. The Department of Justice probably cannot litigate an issue at the moment the agency needs a resolution.

A similar situation can occur at the state level. Agencies in charge of carrying out environmental legislation may lack the authority to prosecute violators. Instead, they must refer violations to the state's attorney general. As it is with the federal government, overseeing referral is difficult. The successful prosecution of a violation may be rare. Because state prosecutory efforts are often directed toward flagrant violations or egregious situations, it is unlikely that water pollution from an AFO will be addressed.

Resources and Personnel

State agencies charged with enforcing regulations can do so only if the legislature has provided them adequate funding. Political and fiscal reasons, however, often leave them without enough funds to enforce existing regulations. Shortages of personnel and equipment for enforcement activities may let violations go unchallenged.

The detailed permit, inspection, and enforcement provisions of some states' AFO provisions require staffs and inspectors. These sometimes exacting regulatory provisions can be quite expensive to implement and enforce. For example, specialized state provisions often require inspections of lagoons and related facilities. As a result, the state may need to provide training to the relevant persons before they can exercise their duties. To inspect an AFO, for example, the inspector will need some knowledge of animal-waste facilities, including design and engineering criteria. In addition, inspectors will need vehicles, and given the scattered locations of operations, they will require considerable time to drive to distant facilities.

Enforcement of nutrient-management programs similarly involves costs and resources. Many state AFO provisions require samples of manure and records of applications. While the logistics and costs of these samples and records have been perfected so that they are reasonable, detecting whether excess nutrients have been applied to any given field presents a more difficult task. Can regulators successfully prosecute farmers for overapplying manure on a field? One case from New York shows that successful prosecution is possible, but it involved a citizen's suit rather than governmental enforcement.[15] Regulatory agencies find it very difficult to garner the time and proof required to establish violations of this sort.

The need for personnel can quickly turn budgets for such enforcement activities into a problem, leaving state-level enforcement agencies insufficient funds for their appointed tasks. Iowa has reported that it employs eighteen persons to work on AFO issues.[16] Given the sparse resources allocated to many agencies charged with enforcing environmental controls, some states may be unable to carry out the inspection and enforcement requirements that their AFO regulations impose.

Willingness to Enforce

Finally, enforcers must be willing and competent to act against violators. When an AFO acts contrary to an antipollution law, will the enforcer impose a sanction adequate to correct the problem? The multitude of independent regulations and obstacles in quantifying enforcement actions make answering this question difficult, but a few enforcement efforts suggest some conclusions and ramifications.

Political or economic pressures often make an agency or official hesitant to enforce pollution regulations. Agricultural interest groups exert considerable influence in some states and may try to relax enforcement measures by political means. In some cases they reduce the enforcement agency's personnel—and hence its capacity—by limiting its budget. In other cases, where an agency attuned to agricultural interests enforces environmental regulations, these groups may influence matters more directly. A state's department of agriculture generally places less emphasis on enforcing an AFO regulation than does its department of environmental protection, and whenever a state's political climate undermines enforcement, at least some AFO operators will likely ignore antipollution rules.

Insufficiently severe penalties introduce yet another enforcement problem. Some penalties amount to little more than a slap on the wrist, providing scant motivation for compliance. For example, a state regulatory department in South Carolina settled a pollution violation involving a wastewater-treatment plant for a mere $100,000, even though the polluter had gained a total economic benefit of more than $1 million.[17]

Enforcement Alternatives

Strict enforcement is not always an optimal response. Agencies sometimes decide to do nothing more than issue a warning letter, a decision not without valid reasons. For example, an agency already working with an operator in establishing meaningful measures to comply with the regulations could decline to take further action. Alternatively, the task of amassing the proof needed to establish the violation may be too formidable. In other situations an agricultural operator's limited resources recommend a warning rather than a fine or injunctive relief.

Some states admit that their enforcement efforts regarding AFO regulations generally do not involve judicial actions. An agency usually has more pressing environmental problems than details concerning an AFO. Whenever one agency handles compliance and another unit handles judicial enforcement actions, few cases reach a litigation stage. For example, in Kansas, where the state attorney general has the authority to levy fines, only about four enforcement actions per year result in fines.[18] States that enable their environmental agencies to assess civil penalties take a more active role in the enforcement of their regulations. Wisconsin reported initiating about fifty enforcement actions a year against unpermitted facilities.[19] North Carolina reported ten actions in a recent year, including two operators that faced criminal charges.[20]

Given the hurdles facing effective enforcement, one might conclude that existing regulatory mechanisms do not sufficiently abate the pollutants produced by AFOs. At some locations the absence of effective regulations, insufficient resources to monitor operations, or an unwillingness to enforce leaves nutrient contamination immune to governmental intervention. Alternative antipollution measures are available, however. Especially helpful are educational programs, demonstrations of voluntary measures, and financial incentives to adopt pollution-reduction technology.

Citizen Suits

Various environmental statutes also allow the use of citizen suits to enforce environmental laws. In citizen suits, individuals act as "private attorneys general." Citizen-suit provisions were added to environmental statutes to help enforce antipollution standards more vigorously. Citizens can initiate litigation themselves, standing in for passive agencies. Citizens can also file suit against the government based on a failure to perform a nondiscretionary duty.

The Clean Water Act enables citizens to bring private enforcement actions. This means that such actions can be brought against CAFOs that are violating federal law. Individuals have the right to sue if they can establish that (1) they have suffered an actual or threatened injury because of the defendant's actions, (2) the injury is "fairly traceable" to the defendant's actions, and (3) the injury will likely be redressed if they prevail in the lawsuit.[21] An organization can sue for its members if some of them are injured. Citizen suits have been authorized in situations where an organization's members claimed harm to aesthetic, environmental, or recreational interests.[22]

Under most citizen-suit provisions, the citizens must notify the alleged violator and responsible enforcement agency at least sixty days prior to filing suit. The sixty-day notice serves two purposes. First, it allows the alleged violator to come into compliance. Second, it allows the agency to step in if enforcement is appropriate.

Citizen suits are not appropriate if an agency is already diligently prosecuting the alleged violator. What constitutes diligent prosecution, however, is not entirely clear. Most courts have held that, to bar a citizen suit, the agency action against the alleged violator must be enforced.[23] The persons bringing citizen suits bear the burden of showing nondiligence by the agency. An agency decision not to prosecute a violation provides no defense against a citizen suit.

For CAFOs, citizen suits are available for the nonenforcement of provisions on permits.[24] Since few CAFOs have secured permits under federal law, citizens have not had many opportunities to address CAFO pollution through citizen suits. A case against an Idaho dairy by the Community Association for Restoration of the Environment resulted in an award of civil penalties of more than \$171,000.[25] Furthermore, the defendant dairy was ordered to pay the plaintiff \$428,304 for costs and attorneys' fees. Other court cases from Indiana[26] and North Carolina[27] show environmental groups assisting states in enforcing provisions of the Clean Water Act.

Litigation suggests that environmental groups are ready and able to challenge violations by CAFOs through citizen-suit actions. Although individual CAFOs may present unique situations that arguably serve as a defense, most cases should be able to be resolved rather quickly. If a CAFO does not have a required permit or is violating a permit, citizens can sue for civil penalties. The new CAFO regulations, which require more operations to secure permits, mean more operations are subject to citizen suits.

Looking for Greater Enforcement

The preceding review of regulations and the activities of regulatory agencies shows some real problems. The data, although incomplete, show AFOs producing unacceptable pollutants. How much of the pollution may be attributed to the absence of meaningful regulations rather than to the violation of existing regulations remains an open question. Clearly, however, both governmental failures in devising appropriate regulatory responses and deficiencies in administering existing regulations have interfered with achieving water-quality goals.

The evidence suggests that we should pursue additional provisions to account for concentrations of pollutants from multiple AFOs in an area and for situations with weighty potentials for pollution. For long-term noncompliant facilities, an additional regulatory mechanism may be needed to bolster compliance. State AFO regulations might benefit from more forceful provisions. Finally, current voluntary controls seem inadequate for unregulated AFOs that disseminate non-point-source pollutants, which might require explicit state regulations for the adoption of appropriate environmental practices.

NOTES

1. Robbin Marks, *Cesspools of Shame: How Factory Farm Lagoons and Sprayfields Threaten Environmental and Public Health* (Washington, D.C.: National Resources Defense Council and the Clean Water Network, 2001), 36.

2. Terence J. Centner, *Legal Structures Governing Animal Waste Management,*

White Papers on Animal Agriculture and the Environment (Raleigh, N.C.: National Center for Manure and Animal Waste Management, 2002), ch. 15.

3. Water Keeper Alliance, Inc., v. Smithfield Foods, Inc., 53 ERC (BNA) 1506; 32 ELR 20320 (2001).

4. State of Iowa v. DeCoster, 596 N.W.2d 898 (Iowa 1999).

5. *Code of Federal Regulations,* title 40, §412.2.

6. Robert Innes, "The Economics of Livestock Waste and Its Regulation," *American Journal of Agricultural Economics* 82 (2000): 97–117.

7. *Maryland Agriculture Code* §§8-704.1, 8-704.2, 8-801–7; *Code of Maryland Regulations,* title 15, subtitle 20.

8. *Minnesota Statutes Annotated* §§17.136, 115.076, 116.06, 116.07; *Minnesota Rules,* ch. 7020.

9. Save the Valley, Inc., v. EPA, 99 F. Supp.2d 981 (S.D. Indiana, Mar. 8, 2000).

10. Environmental Protection Agency, "EPA and Michigan Agree to Protect Water Quality from Manure Runoff," press release no. 02-OPA005 (Chicago: EPA Region 5, 2002).

11. Ken Midkiff, "Taking Big Pig to Court, *The Planet Newsletter* (available at <http://www.sierraclub.org/planet/200110/pig.asp>), Oct. 2001.

12. Water Keeper Alliance v. Smithfield Foods.

13. Daniel Riesel, *Environmental Enforcement Civil and Criminal* (New York: Law Journal Seminars Press, 1996), §1.04(2).

14. Environmental Protection Agency, *State Compendium: Programs and Regulatory Activities Related to Animal Feeding Operations* (Washington, D.C.: EPA, 2001).

15. Concerned Area Residents for the Environment v. Southview Farms, 34 F.2d 114, 118 (2d Cir. 1994).

16. Environmental Protection Agency, *State Compendium: Programs and Regulatory Activities Related to Animal Feeding Operations* (Washington, D.C.: EPA, 1999), IA-9.

17. Friends of the Earth, Inc., v. Laidlaw Environmental Services (TOC), Inc., 120 S. Ct. 693, 707 (2000).

18. EPA, *State Compendium* (1999), KS-7.

19. Ibid., WI-7.

20. Ibid., NC-8.

21. Lujan v. Defenders of Wildlife, 504 U.S. 555, 560–61 (1992).

22. Friends of the Earth v. Laidlaw, 120 S. Ct. at 705 (2000).

23. Janet S. Kole and Stephanie Nye, *Environmental Litigation,* 2d ed. (Chicago: American Bar Association, 1999), 91.

24. Community Association for Restoration of the Environment v. Henry Bosma Dairy, 2001 U.S. Dist. LEXIS 3579 (U.S. District Court, Idaho, Feb. 27, 2001); Idaho Rural Council v. Bosma, 143 F. Supp.2d 1169 (U.S. District Court, Idaho, June 4, 2001).

25. Community Association for Restoration of the Environment v. Henry Bosma Dairy.

26. Save the Valley, Inc., v. EPA, 99 F. Supp.2d 981 (S.D. Indiana, Mar. 8, 2000).

27. Water Keeper Alliance v. Smithfield Foods.

11 Transformations in Food Production

For over thirty years I was able to return to the farm and rekindle my precious childhood memories. With each visit my senses were stimulated to absorb the surroundings, and a rush of memories would engulf my mind. While some things remained the same, however, others gradually changed. Now I view the farm through an overlay of daydreams.

My family arrives at the remodeled farmhouse to visit my parents for a few days. Both my father and grandfather were born in this house. The structure has given the family refuge from the elements for 130 years. Yet the house is not my emotional refuge. I need to walk the farm to achieve the peace I seek with each visit.

As soon as possible, I amble away from the farmhouse, past the barns, and down the old track through the pasture—or rather, the former pasture, since there have been no cows here for thirty years. Two sets of ruts worn into the ground from years of use by tractors and other vehicles avow earlier farm activities. Going downhill I come to Beaver Creek, whose contours I know from countless walks around the farm. Crossing a concrete bridge, I hear the water splash among the rocks as gravity propels it toward its destination. Pausing for a moment, I peer into the waters to look for a fish, frog, or snake.

Turning left, I meander away from the creek. My path takes me upward to avoid an oxbow depression with its steep six-foot bank, a leftover remnant from a bygone course of the creek. After wandering through the former pasture, I mount a small knoll. Again turning left, I continue along the bank above the abandoned streambed for about one hundred feet. I come to the creek. It is silent, the waters being too deep to make any sound. I view the old fishing holes where fish could hide and never be found. Then there are riffles Dad and I used to explore for spawning fish every spring. I recall the frozen creek in the winter. It was usually covered with snow, but on a few occasions when the wind had blown off the snow, I would see how far I could walk on the ice before having to exit to avoid an unfrozen riffle.

It's my family's last summer pilgrimage to the family farm. Rather than daydream by myself, I tell my kids all the stories I can think of. As we walk around the fields, vineyards, and woods and along the creeks, I share accounts of work and activities from the 1960s. I recall experiences with animals, plants, play, snow, floods, and more. I help them envision the farm that I knew . . . And later? We'll all have our own memories of the family's former farm.

Over the past century agriculture has changed tremendously, employing technology and science to increase production and limit environmental degradation. An unscientific, labor-intensive agriculture limited primarily to local markets has evolved into a scientific, computerized, capital-intensive agriculture that markets products globally. As agriculture enters the twenty-first century, how will it keep pace with ongoing changes? Is the agricultural sector in tune with current public opinion, or are agriculturalists lagging behind, pursuing twentieth-century agendas?

Demands for Accountability

Agendas from the last century will not survive because of new public demands for accountability. Although efforts to suppress terrorism may be accompanied by the temporary abeyance of environmental goals, they will someday regain their importance. With pressing fiscal needs both to assure consumers that their food products are safe and to prevent terrorism, our federal government may discontinue current funding programs whereby billions of dollars go to commercial agricultural producers concentrated in a few states. Our country is deeply indebted to our farmers and strongly supports agriculture, but the antiquated current policies and practices cannot be sustained. New regulations and interpretations of laws will reinstate agriculture within the scope of our environment.[1] Rural America will become greener.

Farmers will be told that they do not have a license to damage the environment. Agricultural practices that historically were viewed as the exercise of a landowner's right may no longer be appropriate in today's society. To safeguard public resources and provide health benefits, agricultural producers will have to accept their responsibilities to avoid degrading common air and water resources. They will be expected to help preserve land and water resources for future generations. Agriculture will be forced to become a better neighbor.

At the same time, society should pay for public goods provided by farmers. To ensure "food security" we already support agriculture so that we will continue to have plentiful food reserves. But since we use farmland to clean our air and water resources, why don't we compensate landowners for these services? If lands are used for carbon capture, recreational activities, aesthetic enjoyment, animal and plant habitat protection, waterfowl refuges, or other public purposes, should we not pay the landowners for these beneficial services? Remuneration might take the form of property-tax abatement or a tax credit. Let's develop policies that harvest public goods from farming instead of subsidizing commodity production.

Still, pollution remains a problem, for current regulations have failed to safeguard our land, water, and air resources. Given the health benefits from cleaner air and water and our country's wealth, governments will strive to devise methods to improve the environment. Whereas support for individual legislation dealing with environmental issues varies (and numerous environmental bills fail to become law), the regulatory landscape reveals marked changes. Over the past forty years the industrial sector has learned to survive and prosper under a multitude of command-

and-control statutes and other environmental regulations. Regulations governing wastewater-treatment plants and point-source pollution have eliminated tons of pollutants from our air, land, and waterways. Streams, rivers, and lakes that were once so polluted that they were avoided are now popular resources for recreational activities and habitats for a wide variety of plants and wildlife.

Next on the agenda is agriculture. More agricultural practices will come under governmental regulations. Farmers are aware that they are considered major polluters. Although some farm organizations have dug in their heels, opposing legislative efforts to curb agricultural pollution, their efforts will not prevail. Agriculture is too small a segment of our economy to withstand public pressures for improving environmental quality. Ideas to curb pollution from pesticides, AFOs, and synthetic fertilizers will be introduced into regulations. Fears about bioterrorism, genetically modified organisms, pesticides, and food poisoning will lead legislatures to enact new laws that monitor, control, restrict, and prohibit agricultural activities.

Closer to home, local governments will consider whether crop and animal production involving potential nutrient pollution is consistent with their regions' long-term objectives. Some communities and counties will conclude that safeguarding natural resources, recreational opportunities, and residential quality is more important than allowing crop farms and CAFOs to engage in practices that increase phosphorus, nitrogen, pesticide, and antibiotic loads in soils and waters.

Drawing on Technology and Modeling

Concern about water pollution from excessive amounts of nutrients associated with CAFOs and intensive crop production has led researchers to develop responses to this problem. Two new types of technology in particular will affect specialization and allow regulators to assign pollutants to individual farms. First, precision-farming technology allows us to treat farms as point sources of pollutants, even though they might not be defined as point sources by federal law. Second, computer modeling can forecast pollution for various activities and scenarios to show the efficacy of pollution-control programs. Models can help policy makers recommend new approaches for improving our environment. In turn, prohibitions against polluting activities may alter rural landscapes.

Technology

An increased use of science and technology can help us pinpoint the sources of pollutants. Precision-farming technology, involving remote sensing, variable-rate technology, and positioning satellite imagery, is allowing farmers to map their field conditions. In turn, mapping information provides data for decisions on inputs. Farmers can limit amounts of fertilizer, pesticides, and water to those needed for optimal production.

Precision-farming technology might similarly help regulators determine which farmers are straying from acceptable practices. Descriptive geographical information-system applications use information about farmers' and nutrients' locations to show environmental impacts. Precision-farming technology and geographical information-system applications will let regulators assign pollutants to their sources more accurately, distinguishing not only among fields and farms but also among pollutants from animals and those from commercial fertilizers and other sources. With such specificity, regulators can manage actual rather than potential pollution.

Regulators thus have an opportunity to use technology to devise regulations that incorporate considerable detail yet have the flexibility to handle different conditions. For example, technology can be employed to prohibit the application of manure when agronomic information shows excess amounts of nitrogen or phosphorus in the ground. Other rules could limit manure application to times when it is likely that plants would use the nutrients. In this manner, fewer nutrients would be available to impair waters.

Modeling

The appropriate use of modeling systems can help producers and other firms eliminate the release of excessive pollutants into the environment. Several major modeling systems have been used to assess conditions contributing to water impairment, including excess nitrogen and phosphorus from CAFOs and intensely farmed acreages. Through modeling and subsequent predictions, experts are tying the costs of excessive nutrients to persons responsible for placing the nutrients in the environment. Furthermore, other modeling systems can identify policy measures for improving water quality, such as recommending a tax on pollutants or granting incentives to reduce pollution.

Scientists have developed a phosphorus index that can serve as a tool to assess landforms and management practices for estimating the potential risk of phosphorus movement to water bodies.[2] Farmers can use the index to prioritize fields for the application of manure and to identify fields on which more careful management of phosphorus is imperative. Legislators might use this index to reduce phosphorus movement and probable water-quality degradation, requiring conservation and phosphorus-management practices whenever a site has a "high" or "very high" rating.

Finally, modeling has been used to structure financial incentives that encourage reductions in the deployment of nutrients. Governments can implement incentives by making funds available for technical expertise or for the adoption of structural elements to reduce nutrient pollution. Governmental incentives have helped farmers develop fertilizer plans and comprehensive nutrient-management plans, construct animal-waste retention structures, and transport nutrients out of a watershed.

Developing and Applying Regulations

Governments can do more to reduce all types of non-point-source pollution and potential health hazards. Regulations play their part, but they must be enforced. For agricultural producers, BMPs offer an additional mechanism to improve environmental quality. Still, although we have the resources and technology to address non-point-source pollution more effectively, we need to learn more about its origins. If CAFOs are major polluters, let's augment the controls on them. If other sources (such as storm-sewer overflows and construction activities) are the offenders, let's regulate those sectors. Significantly, efforts to control environmental damages routinely miss one nonagricultural source: manicured recreational facilities (e.g., golf courses) and suburban lawns that employ significant quantities of pesticides and fertilizers to maintain their lush greenery and visual appeal.

Encouraging BMPs

Experiences with BMPs show that, although they may not solve nutrient-pollution problems entirely, they can intercept pollutants from fertilizers and animal waste to avoid the impairment of waters. Farms without a nutrient-management system should be a priority. Animal manure or waste can be placed in lagoons, retention ponds, or storage structures until it can be applied effectively as a fertilizer. Nutrient-management plans help producers use nutrients in agricultural production rather than let them run off into streams and water bodies.

Legislators and agencies need to work with farmers at where they are to reduce unacceptable pollution.[3] Better information and technology will help farmers reduce their contamination. For example, some farmers are learning how to apply less nitrogen fertilizer and still achieve desired corn yields.[4] Others still need assistance in learning how to regulate nutrient applications to plant needs and coordinate the application of animal waste and fertilizers to reduce pollution from excess nutrients.

Some areas of our country are home to native species that can protect soil resources and extend water availability. Native prairie species growing and maturing at different times can use solar energy from early spring until after the last frost.[5] Such species might offer more protection to the soil and slow the movement of water into streams.[6] Further efforts at introducing crop rotations where native species were sometimes planted on fields could reduce dependence on synthetic fertilizers and pesticides.

Another priority should be the continued emphasis on fencing, filter strips, grassed waterways, cover crops, and riparian buffers. By keeping crop production and animals away from streams and water bodies, operators can reduce the amounts of nutrients that enter these waters. The vegetative sinks intercept nutrients, so they do not enter the water as pollutants. Because many farms have not fully developed these BMPs, financial incentives may be helpful. Alternatively, new provisions might make these practices mandatory in enumerated situations.

Moving beyond Command and Control

Perhaps the greatest challenge for policy makers is to develop more discerning regulations to reduce pollution. The command-and-control strategies so often used for point-source pollution offer only a beginning point; without more, they do not offer a satisfactory response to most non-point-source pollution problems. In addition, although such standards can be effective in reducing pollution, they often unnecessarily burden operators who are not contributing to a pollution problem. Many regulations also prescribe specific technology rather than set performance standards. Such regulations block innovation and the adoption of superior technology.

Our governments are not heeding the economic lessons gained from their years of experience with overly costly point-source pollution abatement efforts, which have shown the inefficiency of foisting expenses on nonpolluters. Yet that is exactly what governmental regulators are doing in their responses to animal waste. Rather than use technology and science to identify polluters and control actual pollution, the regulations restrain businesses. Regulators are subjugating CAFOs to permitting prerequisites, paperwork, and pollution-prevention projects based on numbers of animals without considering whether they are part of a pollution problem.

Science-based Specifics

Legislatures and regulators should use scientific findings to avoid casting too wide a net, for there may be little need to regulate practices and operations unlikely to cause pollution. Not all CAFOs with a given number of animals beget nutrient contamination, and some types of crop production are less likely to cause environmental problems than others. In addition, farms located where they do not impair waters may not need to be subject to the same requirements as are others. Such overregulation and its attendant costs penalize farmers who are not causing problems. By devising more specific controls that regulate only those operations that harm the environment, we might lower costs for agricultural producers.

We can be more creative in devising responses to the environmental problems generated by all sources. Precision-farming technology, geographical information-systems technology, and modeling can be used to target specific watersheds, selected practices, and offensive operations. Existing technology can let us regulate not firms but only situations where unacceptable pollution occurs. This will allow us to achieve productivity gains while reducing pollutants. Furthermore, science-based regulations can lead to product and service prices that more accurately reflect associated environmental costs.

Trends for the Coming Decade

What do the changes in agricultural production mean for our country, our rural areas, and firms that service agriculture? Plenty. Until we embark on new, unconventional policies, our agriculture will become more segmented. Areas and regions will acquire more specialized production activities and facilities. Rural areas without an influx of urbanites or retirees will continue to depopulate and wither. Firms will consolidate and close small facilities with a ruthless fixation on efficiency. Economics is a harsh taskmaster. As agriculture becomes industrialized, the individual players will not garner much consolation. Although federal programs attempt to support certain commodities and activities, some farmers and firms will not survive.

Federal conservation programs are important, but we have other opportunities to improve the quality of our environment. Our legislative and regulatory representatives can draw on many options to develop new responses to contemporary pollution problems. The choices are not simple, and flawed responses will have bothersome consequences. I offer five predictions for the first decade of the third millennium c.e.: (1) we will see more regulations enacted, (2) non-point-source pollution will present difficulties in devising regulations, (3) conflicts over land uses will increase, (4) agricultural operations will continue to specialize, and (5) consumers will embrace "environmentally friendly" food products.

More Regulations

Regulators will adopt additional environmental regulations at all levels of government. There are no secrets here. Given its desire for cleaner air and water, society will support a more efficacious environmental agenda. The 9/11 terrorist attacks and the subsequent economic woes may overshadow environmental issues temporarily, but they remain on the back burner for another day. People value their health, so they want a reduction in all types of contamination. Given agriculture's small population base, our plentiful food supplies, and the acknowledged pollution from agricultural activities, governments can do more to force polluters to comply with current laws. The EPA will seek to regulate a greater percentage of the waste produced by animals, states will continue with their responses to existing pollutants, and local governments will respond to community problems.

Some governments may be ready to move to a more comprehensive set of regulatory provisions that more accurately account for benefits and costs of land uses. An "environmental benefits index" might help regulations factor in the use of stewardship practices. Governmental restrictions and monetary assistance programs might be connected to public policy objectives and environmental goals. A broader "farm results index" could form the basis for supporting landowners who are providing public goods.[7] This index could consider landowner efforts supporting biodiversity, wetland protection, water protection, and other factors.

If Americans want a cleaner environment, they cannot be complacent. They have to make sure their governments hear their voices. The powerful lobbying campaign by agribusiness organizations decrying our farmers' dire financial straits competes with the environmental agenda. Health benefits offer the justification for most of the new regulatory proposals. By relating environmental degradation to public health problems, it will be possible to implement additional safeguards to secure a more wholesome environment.

Mechanisms to Regulate Non-Point-Source Pollution

Current levels of non-point-source pollution are unacceptable. While the diffuse nature of and differences among pollutants make their regulation difficult, new technology will pave the way for more appropriate responses. CAFOs, other farming operations, construction sites, and additional nonpoint pollution sources will be subjected to new regulations. Regulators may select total maximum daily loads or use command-and-control mechanisms to achieve this reduction.

We will be shortsighted, however, if we limit the options to these mechanisms. Less costly alternative practices can help reduce non-point-source pollutants. In some cases additional educational programs are needed to help operators adopt voluntary BMPs. Financial incentives for greater efforts to intercept pollutants can lead to reductions of pollutants as well. Increased funding for enforcement efforts can reduce contamination, too, since many governments have lacked the money or staff to enforce existing regulations. In fact, more vigorous enforcement of current regulations might dissipate the need to enact additional regulations. Ultimately, we will need to draw on several approaches to help reduce unacceptable pollutants.

Outdated environmental requirements will no doubt persist, but if we heed the lessons learned from point-source pollution regulations, we can implement more cost-efficient environmental controls. Over time we will move toward more flexible approaches that more accurately address specific problems.

Conflicts with Urbanites

Conflicts over land use occur in many areas. Agriculture will continue to be pressured by incompatible urban and recreational pursuits. Forty years ago most people who lived outside cities had some connection to (or appreciation for) farming. Farms were everywhere, and people had an uncle or a grandfather who owned or worked on a farm. Today those connections are gone. Most people have no idea what agriculture involves. Even many agricultural scientists and persons working for agribusiness firms lack personal knowledge of agricultural production.

This disconnection means that most people will not tolerate the offensive odors and disagreeable activities associated with agricultural endeavors. Environmental requirements will limit agricultural production in some locations. States and communities that place a high value on residential, recreational, and other activities will take action to eliminate agricultural pursuits. Through zoning, health ordinances, and safety requirements, we will erode the competitiveness of agricultural producers, leading some to abandon their farming pursuits.

Specialization

With our excellent transportation system and the economies of scale that accompany specialization, agricultural operations will gravitate to areas with cost advantages. Surpluses of food will continue to drive down agricultural commodity prices, presenting farmers a tough row to hoe. Simple economics will drive small and unprofitable producers out of business. Costs of new technology and regulatory expenses will encourage specialization and lead to the demise of some farms.

We also might expect some types of agricultural production to migrate to Third World countries. As countries' per-capita incomes increase, so too do their labor costs and citizens' demands for environmental quality. The higher labor costs and more demanding environmental regulations of the United States may offer producers in other (especially Third World) countries a competitive advantage. As Third World producers gain such advantages, some types of agricultural activities will shift to these countries.

Food Safety and "Eco-Friendly" Products

A considerable number of consumers are concerned about their health and want to improve environmental quality. The demand for safe food will alter agricultural production and marketing. Governmental regulations will be subjected to scrutiny and modified to streamline the system of safety controls. Innovative regulatory and industry programs will require practices that make food products less likely to carry pathogens or other harmful substances. Other responses will provide information to dispel consumer fears. Concerns about foot-and-mouth disease and bovine spongiform encephalopathy (BSE) will lead to new responses to assure consumers that meat products are safe.

A growing number of Americans are supporting environmental quality by purchasing "environmentally friendly" products. This trend is even more pronounced in Europe. Marketers have begun to promote products by labeling and advertising them in ways that extol their environmental virtues. This technique, first known as "green labeling" and now more commonly called "eco-labeling," has rapidly become an established technique. Devices such as organic certification and ISO 14000 standards, developed by the International Standards Organization, let consumers support environmentally friendly products and companies. The evolution of additional information systems to denote eco-friendly products and production methods will make more options available. We will see a flourishing market for eco-friendly products, and producers who cater to this market will be able to reap financial rewards.

Strive for Equitable Responses

Our country has taken great steps toward fairness in the regulation of people and businesses, and the principles of equality we devised in doing so should apply to pollution legislation as well. In proposing its CAFO regulations in 2001, however, the EPA raised significant questions about equity. Considerable pollution enters our waters from wastewater-treatment plants, storm sewers, construction sites, overfertilized suburban lawns, and golf courses. Were CAFOs being unfairly targeted? Do more equitable solutions exist for responding to nutrient pollution?

One justification for further regulating CAFOs has been to reduce their capacity to harm the environment during natural disasters such as floods, as happened in North Carolina. Hurricane Floyd inundated approximately 50 waste lagoons at hog farms, the contents from 5 lagoons were released into the flood waters, and the hurricane killed nearly 3 million domestic animals. These same floods damaged 209 sewage plants,[8] however, and washed 129 caskets from the ground at flooded cemeteries.[9]

Given the numerous potential sources of contamination during events such as hurricanes, we simply can't prevent all pollution. Natural disasters and emergencies will be accompanied by pollutant discharges. Appropriate planning and regulatory requirements can lessen damages from natural disasters, but they must factor in economic components, risks, and the potential for damages. Occasionally, the risk of environmental degradation is so remote that a rational response is not to do anything. Moreover, we need consistent policy for all polluters, agricultural as well as municipal and industrial facilities.

Because it covers a greater area than urban and suburban sites do, agriculture may generate more contaminants, yet this provides no reason to treat it more harshly than other sources of pollutants. On a per-acre basis, golf courses, construction sites, and highway projects often generate more pollutants than agriculture does. Moreover, nonagricultural sites may contribute more harmful pollution. Highways, parking lots, and other paved areas are known to release petroleum products, heavy metals, phosphorus, bacteria, and pet feces into our water resources.

Among point sources, many combined sewer overflows discharge untreated human sewage into rivers and lakes when there are heavy rains. Can we reconcile provisions sanctioning municipal overflows with requirements that CAFO lagoons be designed to have no discharges except for twenty-five- or one-hundred-year rainfall events? What about pollution from commercial fertilizers? We may want to employ similar standards for all sources of a given pollutant. Indicators on the origin of waste products can help us discern the sources of pollutants. Once we identify those sources, we can develop evenhanded provisions to preclude nutrients from damaging our environment.

Since phosphorus and nitrogen often are a problem, we might attempt to devise a more comprehensive program that regulates all their sources. One idea drawn from pesticide-collection programs is to employ a nutrient tax.[10] The tax could be applied to all sources of a particular nutrient that is damaging the environment. Funds collected from nutrient taxes could be used to finance pollution-reduction incentive programs, invest in technology for reducing nutrient contamination, or subsidize remedial measures for reducing concentrations of nutrients.

NOTES

1. Beth E. Waterhouse, "A Refined Taste in Natural Objects," in *The Farm as a Natural Habitat: Reconnecting Food Systems with Ecosystems,* ed. Dana L. Jackson and Laura L. Jackson (Washington, D.C.: Island, 2002), 236.

2. U.S. Department of Agriculture, *Technical Note: The Phosphorus Index: A Phosphorus Assessment Tool,* Natural Resources Conservation Service, Engineering Series, no. 1901 (Washington, D.C.: USDA, 1994).

3. Rhonda R. Janke, "Composing a Landscape," in *The Farm as a Natural Habitat,* ed. Jackson and Jackson, 219.

4. Brian A. DeVore, "Nature's Backlash," in *The Farm as a Natural Habitat,* ed. Jackson and Jackson, 34.

5. Laura L. Jackson, "Restoring Prairie Processes to Farmlands," in *The Farm as a Natural Habitat,* ed. Jackson and Jackson, 142.

6. Ibid., 142.

7. George M. Boody, "Agriculture as a Public Good," in *The Farm as a Natural Habitat,* ed. Jackson and Jackson, 272.

8. Cable News Network, "Floyd's Legacy: Record Losses in North Carolina" (available at <http://www.CNN.com>), Sept. 22, 1999.

9. Associated Press, "More Rain Prolongs Misery in North Carolina" (available at <http://www.USAtoday.com>), Sept. 29, 1999.

10. Terence J. Centner and Lewell F. Gunter, "Financing the Disposal of Unwanted Agricultural Pesticides," *Environment International* 25 (1999): 635–46.

12 Plowing Forward to a Cleaner Environment

I miss the countryside I once knew. My daily chores, commencing before school, may have been tedious, but they were wholesome and productive. They gave me a valuable work ethic often missing from today's society: you did what you were told to do, did it without complaining, and did it well. Work was done before play. Chores such as milking cows, feeding animals, or harvesting hay had to be done in a timely fashion.

Our community and the rural institutions in our lives existed at a scale conducive to a good life. My cousins lived on farms only a few miles away, and we had many opportunities to play together and become good friends. For major holidays, Mom would plan how to include both her family and Dad's in our celebrations. But it wasn't just family; up the road lived a widowed neighbor whom Mom would invite to dinner almost once a month, and we all enjoyed sharing our lives with this active and engaging person.

I belonged to a 4-H club and enjoyed weekly activities with friends who had similar interests. At monthly club meetings we practiced leadership skills as we organized fundraisers, community-service projects, and social activities. We sponsored a community ice-cream social, tended to rose bushes in a local park, and had a "family harvest" supper each fall. Parents with special talents volunteered to teach children through 4-H projects. My dad taught the tractor project, and Mom led horticultural projects.

We knew the people from whom we bought supplies and to whom we made calls for services. When we accompanied Dad to the local farm-supply store, we could explore the warehouses and view the intriguing stock for sale. If a tractor wouldn't start, a neighboring mechanic would fix it. Our local veterinarian was always on call and would come to the farm whenever we had a sick cow. A milk tester came every month to weigh the milk produced by each cow and determine the milk's butterfat content.

Summers were a working holiday. We seemed always to have farm chores that had to be done. Long hours were spent helping Dad cut and bale hay, weeding the vegetable garden, and helping Mom pick and preserve vegetables. Like all children, we occasionally balked, and my parents had to push us to do some of these chores. I particularly remember that I disliked hoeing weeds, and this task was used as punishment for misdeeds. Nonetheless, I received tremendous satisfaction from tending to the vegetable garden, overcoming pests and droughts, and reaping its harvests. Still, we did have time to explore the neighboring woods and creeks. I remember searching for fish and looking for bird nests. On hikes along the creek floodplain and through the woods I would search for new plants and observe the different habitats.

Agriculture will continue to evolve, and our rural countryside will continue to change. Rural dwellers will notice the transformation and may lament bygone features they were accustomed to seeing and enjoying. Those of us who remember the countryside from forty or more years ago will likely berate the circumstances that have led to the demise of the bucolic America we loved. Although we may seek to return, however, there is no way to go back. And indeed, the rural America of the 1960s, or of prior generations, was not the utopia we conjure in our memories. Rural America of the 1960s involved hard work, low wages, and polluting activities.

Today, while much of our rural countryside may appear healthy, the threats that accompany concentrated activities and divergences from sustainable practices lie hidden. Concentrations of animals have increased nutrient pollution, and specialization in crop production requires tons of pesticides and artificial fertilizers. Because these practices harm our soil resources, they are leading many people to advocate additional environmental regulations. Increased regulation might threaten farmers financially, but the modest increases in food prices would be justified by health benefits and the preservation of soil and water resources.

Enacting regulations is not the only way to improve the countryside. Even existing regulations do no good if they are not enforced, as is often the case. Incentives come into play, too. Should we continue with existing programs that encourage intensive cultivation, or can we devise new programs with effective relationships between money paid to farmers and societal objectives? Perhaps we can use alternative programs to more vigorously encourage activities that enhance rural communities.

The conditions of one's youth cannot persist. Our world differs from that of our parents. The farms and perceived vibrant communities of earlier generations cannot be revived. No matter what governments do and how much money society commits, we will not stop growth or preserve the small farms of yesteryear. Progress is change. Yet this does not prevent us from trying to improve our countryside. We can identify innovative policies that offer greater support to our rural communities and enhance rural America.

A Few Additional Costs for Significant Benefits

Our environmental achievements cost money; there is no free ride. Stopping environmental damage and cleaning up polluted sites are expensive. Over the past few decades we have heard numerous complaints about the costs involved in complying with environmental regulations and arguments that specific laws are so expensive they should be repealed. Other arguments assert that environmental requirements are excessive or unnecessary. Yet most such rules respond to real problems and provide significant benefits. By curtailing the disposal of carcinogens, environmental laws have been fundamental in abating health problems, and the reduction of pollutants in our environment has lowered medical expenses significantly.

Moreover, our environmental regulations and the consequent improvements in water and air quality have meant lower costs for persons and firms using natural resources as inputs for producing goods. Other benefits of our nation's environmental laws include the conservation of natural resources, heightened recreational opportunities, discoveries of more cost-efficient technology, and new jobs. We also endorse some environmental regulations to preserve habitats and stop the extermination of species. These benefits suggest that proposals to eliminate an environmental control or exempt an industry from existing environmental regulations may be shortsighted.

As regulation and accountability increase, however, agricultural production will become more expensive. For example, if AFOs cannot freely allow waste to dissipate into streams or the air, they will need to establish alternative—and more expensive—disposal methods. The EPA predicted that its proposed CAFO regulation would result in a 1–2 percent rise in retail food prices.[1] Fencing animals from a stream along one side of a square 100–acre field (20,900 feet of fence) costs about $26,125 ($1.25 per linear foot).[2] A dairy producer needing to construct an animal-waste lagoon for a herd of 150–300 animals will have to spend more than $22,000.[3]

These figures suggest significant costs, but research on nutrient-management legislation for the poultry industry showed that regulations should not pose a significant barrier to the industry's continued survival.[4] Moreover, the increased production costs would not cause food prices to rise that much. The farm value of animal-derived food products is only 30–43 percent of their retail price.[5] Even if environmental requirements increased production costs by 20 percent, retail prices for animal-derived food products would increase by only 6–9 percent. Since beef, pork, poultry, other meats, dairy products, and eggs constitute about 33 percent of our food costs,[6] a 20 percent increase in animal-production costs might increase overall food costs only about 2–3 percent. Food costs in the United States and most of the developed world are low. We can afford additional requirements to safeguard the environment.

Augment Enforcement Efforts

The obstacles to achieving water-quality goals include more than insufficient regulatory responses. Failures to enforce existing regulations have played an equally important role, letting polluters flout the laws. For example, the EPA found that a majority of CAFOs had not secured NPDES permits as required under the Clean Water Act.[7] We lack effective and efficient enforcement of pollution regulations for several reasons. First, the federal government assigns enforcement responsibilities to states but does little to ensure that they are carried out. Second, political and economic pressures have meant lapses in enforcement. Third, both state and federal regulatory agencies lack the resources or personnel to meet their enforcement responsibilities. Fourth, regulatory agencies may be distracted from enforcing CAFO regulations. We should address all these issues, increasing oversight of the agencies charged with controlling pollution from CAFOs, demanding that our governments enforce existing laws, and adequately funding the relevant agencies.

Ineffective enforcement penalizes environmentally conscientious farmers. They spend money to comply with environmental laws while violators continue to pollute. This pollution from unauthorized sources in turn leads governments to overregulate, for citizens and regulators see it as a justification to advance even more stringent controls. Because of a few violators and their contamination of water resources, an entire industry may be subjected to additional, excessive regulations. A more nuanced approach could help. Further efforts at monitoring pollutants, incorporating technological discoveries into regulations and dealing with tangible rather than projected problems, can facilitate reductions in pollutants without penalizing good operators.

Matching Governmental Policy with Rural Needs

Our federal government has limited funds available for agriculture. Disappointments in various conservation programs has tempered some of the support for continued environmental funding, but the biggest obstacle is the farm lobby. Our large marketing firms, bankers, major farm organizations, and factory farmers would rather have public funds flow to farmers as commodity price supports than to rural communities for environmental, public-health, and recreational projects.

The controversy involves whether we should assist agriculture by subsidizing producers of enumerated commodities—such as wheat, soybeans, corn, cotton, and sugar—or by funding other endeavors in rural areas. Money flows to beneficiaries in both scenarios, but if we elect to support commodities, the funds will probably not reach rural communities. One-half of 1999's farm payments were distributed in six states; that year more than one-half of our $16 billion farm payments went to the largest 8 percent of our farms.[8] A governmental commodity-support program that mainly subsidizes large producers of a few crops does not effectively champion the human qualities of rural communities. Moreover, increasing such subsidies will reduce the money available for environmental and other rural programs. Current federal farm programs subsidize agriculture but not rural America.

When drafting the 2002 farm bill, Congress had a once-in-a-lifetime opportunity to support agriculture through incentives designed to further conservation, food-safety, health, environmental-protection, and rural-development goals. Everyone agreed on our country's need to provide assistance to rural America but not on the form the support should take. Rather than link agricultural-support programs to infrastructural development, the farm lobby successfully supported industrial agriculture and a return to commodity price supports. The 2002 farm bill is expected to shunt one-half of our governmental support payments to corporations and industrial-sized farms.

We have choices. Rather than worry about numbers of farms or low commodity prices due to overproduction, let's try to bolster rural communities. We need to "reverse the siphon that has for so long been drawing resources, money, talent, and people from our countryside."[9] Rather than strive for efficiency, we need to consider sufficiency.[10] Through thoughtful new programs, we can direct money and other resources to infrastructural development and communities, not the selected producers of a few favored commodities.

Enhancement Suggestions for Rural America

Our government's decision to support our largest farms at the expense of smaller family farms is not above reproach. Drawing on the practices and characteristics of the smaller, more diverse farms of yesteryear, we can confront the ecological, social, and cultural problems plaguing agriculture today.[11] By identifying positive policies quite different from those that have emerged over the past few decades, we can develop a better rural America.

What was important to our agricultural communities of the 1960s? Was it the small farms or something else? A little reflection shows that the important factor was not the diminutive size of the farms but rather the communities that emerged around farm-based economies, places where people could acquire neighborly values during times when many people remained rooted in one place.[12] These conditions facilitated social ties, affections, tolerance, generosity, and community service.[13] Thus, policies supporting small farms have merit. We should support agronomic pursuits that can be practiced on small holdings, but must realize that economies of scale will limit this policy.

If we want to help revitalize rural communities, we need to assist residents in local enterprises and provide more money for sustaining these communities and their activities. We can attempt to do this through governmental programs that invest in the infrastructures of rural communities and pump money into the rural economy. For the greatest effect, funds need to end up with persons living in these communities. Funds paid to absentee landlords or agribusiness firms in neighboring or distant cities do not bolster local rural economies.

We might also strive to develop elements that would allow local communities to sustain themselves. Rural areas do more than produce food for our tables and for export; they also help provide cleaner air and water resources, public health and food security, and sites for recreational pursuits. We can thus help reinvigorate rural communities by devising innovative programs that direct funds to landowners and communities in exchange for these services.

Cleaner Air and Water Resources

Support for environmental programs that advance cleaner air and water is hardly new. Governments have taken an active role in helping farmers become better stewards of our natural resources since the 1930s. Over several decades our federal government has continued these efforts with a variety of programs that have assisted farmers with adopting practices to reduce pollution or limit environmental degradation. Further consideration of educational programs, technical assistance, and financial assistance is appropriate. Today's challenge is not only to continue with existing programs but also to target the most egregious problems for funding and to expand support for additional stewardship practices.

Industrial and commercial firms treat the disposal of their waste as a production cost. Agriculture and other waste generators can be held to similar standards. The current situation, in which so many streams and water bodies remain impaired, shows that our contemporary regulations are insufficient. We must do more to reduce water pollution, especially by helping polluters find ways to abate pollutants. State legislatures that have not fully considered options to address all sources of nutrient pollution are shortsighted in the management of their resources and remiss in their duties to ensure the future safety of their constituents.

Public Health and Food Security

We might petition governments for agricultural programs that are more supportive of public health and food security. We are told that the diets of millions of Americans could be improved through the consumption of more fresh fruit and vegetable products. Nevertheless, grain and crop producers receive nearly all our agricultural subsidies, with this assistance indirectly supporting animal products through cheaper feed grains. Other subsidies are less direct. We subsidize transportation through our military expenditures protecting oil supplies in the Middle East and federal highway funds. Our petroleum prices fail to account for their true costs, thus subsidizing agricultural practices dependent on petroleum-based products. Our governmental policies are encouraging cultivation, the overuse of commercial fertilizers, and movement of grains and food products to distant markets. Rather than subsidize transportation, grain, and animal products, why don't we offer more support for sustainable production practices and fruits and vegetables?

Producing fruits and vegetables locally could have a number of benefits. First, the operations would tend to be small, more like family farms. Additionally, this idea moves us toward a local food supply, generally considered to be the safest.[14] Local suppliers make it easier to monitor pesticides and ensure the continued safety of the products. Whereas we now subsidize grains and meat products for export, we might alter farm programs and redirect federal commodity funds to support locally grown fruit and vegetable products.

Recreational Pursuits and Retirement Activities

Finally, we might seek to reinvigorate the countryside by supporting its use for recreation and leisure activities. Hiking, biking, birding, and camping are pastimes suited for the countryside. Why not support programs that would provide funds to rural landowners and communities associated with the development of hiking and biking trails or campgrounds? We might also assist in the development of countryside initiatives for retirees. These additional social and recreational activities would entice more people to the countryside and cause a corresponding need for additional services, which could bring money into local economies.

Returning to the Countryside

The absence of animals in our countryside is not likely to change. Given the economic advantages that accompany large-scale agricultural production, we probably will not see the return of multiple animal species to commercial farms. Yet the absence of green pastures need not be accompanied by pollution or even remain an entrenched feature of our rural environment. We can take measures to improve our air and water resources and to bring more people to rural areas. I suggest nine opportunities for revitalizing rural landscapes.

1. *Make it uneconomic to pollute.* Too many people are polluting because of the lack of a penalty. Regulate pollutants, not agribusinesses. Mandate financial penalties and remedial actions for producers and firms that degrade our water and air resources. In some cases, tax pollutants and use the funds to address related pollution problems.

2. *Provide incentives for cleaning air and water resources.* Air and water are public goods. Create additional programs to assist persons who adopt activities or mechanisms that intercept pollutants before they enter water and air resources. Expand programs to reward landowners already providing public benefits.

3. *Fund regulatory enforcement.* Regulators fail to detect many of the pollutants being discharged into our waterways and air. Encourage legislative bodies to provide the necessary funding so that regulators can prosecute violators.

4. *Enforce existing regulations.* Too many polluters are not being prosecuted. Hold governmental regulators to the law, or expand citizen-suit provisions to assist governments in enforcing the law so that violators are more likely to be punished.

5. *Direct funds to communities rather than commodities.* Current federal programs direct a disproportionate share of funds to selected commodities. Fund infrastructural development programs to funnel money to rural America instead of bolstering overproduction through commodity price supports.

6. *Champion small-scale operations and activities.* Current federal programs subsidize large commercial producers above all others. Amend agricultural programs to channel more funds to smaller operations. Offer incentives for sustainable production practices.

7. *Foster recreational and leisure activities in the countryside.* Attract more people to rural communities. Activities such as hiking, camping, and bird-watching can attract people to rural areas. Provide incentives or programs to assist with the development of these activities.

8. *Support locally grown food products.* Locally grown products support rural communities. Develop mechanisms or programs that encourage the production of local fruits and vegetables.

9. *Assist local governments with governance.* Local governments often need help in devising appropriate local controls. Through educational programs, model ordinances, and grant programs, provide information to local governments to help them address environmental and community issues more successfully.

The transformations of rural America offer significant options. As in navigating the Internet or selecting new software, more than one approach will work. By acknowledging the changes that have occurred, we can try various options until we find those that best address our concerns about rural America. By searching for different solutions, we can advance regulations that support agricultural production, rural communities, and cleaner air and water resources. If we make the proper choices and act prudently, our rural landscapes can be even more magnificent than those of our ancestors.

The nine suggestions for rejuvenating rural landscapes serve as paradigms for programs that can curtail pollutants and improve the rural environment. Of course, there will be obstacles no matter which approach we select. The biotech industry, agribusiness lobby, and commodity groups exert tremendous power over the legislative process. They will pursue programs that will compete with ours. Yet we have come a long way in addressing point-source pollution and other problems; we can do the same for non-point-source pollution. The nine suggestions provide us opportunities to navigate toward a cleaner environment and to design tools for the optimal use of governmental assistance. It is up to us to provide greater direction to regulators and entrust them with appropriate resources so that they can design a better rural America.

NOTES

1. Environmental Protection Agency, "National Pollutant Discharge Elimination System Permit Regulation and Effluent Limitations Guidelines and Standards for Concentrated Animal Feeding Operations; Proposed Rule," *Federal Register* 66 (Jan. 12, 2001): 3093.

2. Keith O. Keplinger and Bryan DeBose, *Costs and Environmental Effectiveness for Nutrient BMPs* (Stephenville, Tex.: Tarleton State University, 1998), 19.

3. "Dairy Farmers Having Success Piping Animal Waste to Lagoons," *Water Engineering and Management* 147, no. 8 (Aug. 2000): 18; Keplinger and DeBose, *Costs and Environmental Effectiveness,* 23.

4. C. S. McIntosh, T. A. Park, and C. Karnum, "The Potential Impact of Imposing Best Management Practices for Nutrient Management on the US Broiler Industry," *Journal of Environmental Management* 60 (2000): 145–54.

5. U.S. Department of Agriculture, *Agricultural Statistics 2000* (Washington, D.C.: USDA), IX-26.

6. U.S. Department of Agriculture, "Food and Marketing," *Agricultural Outlook* (Washington, D.C.: Economic Research Service, 2001), 21.

7. Environmental Protection Agency, "Proposed Rule," 3080.

8. General Accounting Office, *Farm Programs: Information on Recipients of Federal Payments,* GAO-01-606 (Washington, D.C.: GAO, 2001).

9. Wendell Berry, *Another Turn of the Crank* (Washington, D.C.: Counterpoint, 1995), 24.

10. Wes Jackson, *Becoming Native to This Place* (Lexington: University Press of Kentucky, 1994), 60.

11. Wendell Berry, "The Death of the Rural Community," *The Ecologist* 29 (May–June 1999): 183–84.

12. Carl D. Esbjornson, "Does Community Have a Value?—A Reply," in *Rooted in the Land,* ed. William Vitek and Wes Jackson (New Haven, Conn.: Yale University Press, 1996), 92.

13. Ibid., 92.

14. Berry, *Another Turn,* 6.

Appendix 1: Regulatory Agencies for Animal Feeding Operations

Alabama Department of Environment Management
Field Operations Division
P.O. Box 301463
Montgomery, AL 36130
Telephone: 334-394-4326
Web: <http://www.adem.state.al.us/Regulations/regulations.htm>

Alaska (permitting authority is with the federal government)
US EPA Region 10
1200 Sixth Avenue
Seattle, WA 98101-1128
Telephone: 206-553-1448
Web: <http://yosemite.epa.gov/R10/ecocomm.nsf/0/
9e603fef1cccdcf9882569d90079cf55?OpenDocument>

Arizona Department of Environmental Quality
Water Quality Division
1110 West Washington Street
Phoenix, AZ 85007
Telephone: 602-771-4651
Web: <http://www.adeq.state.az.us/environ/water/index.html>

Arkansas Department of Environmental Quality
Division of Water
8001 National Drive
Little Rock, AR 72219
Telephone: 501-682-0616
Web: <http://www.adeq.state.ar.us/water/default.htm>

California State Water Resources Control Board
(and Regional Water Quality Control Boards)
1001 I Street
Sacramento, CA 95814
Telephone: 916-341-5587
Web: <http://www.swrcb.ca.gov/>

Colorado Department of Public Health and Environment
Water Quality Control Division
4300 Cherry Creek Drive South
Denver, CO 80246
Telephone: 303-692-3520
Web: <http://www.cdphe.state.co.us/wq/wqhom.asp>

Connecticut Department of Environmental Protection
Bureau of Water Management
79 Elm Street
Hartford, CT 06106-5127
Telephone: 860-424-3701
Web: <http://dep.state.ct.us/wtr/>

Delaware Department of Natural Resources and Environmental Control
Division of Water Resources
P.O. Box 1401
89 Kings Highway
Dover, DE 19901
Telephone: 302-739-4860
Web: <http://www.dnrec.state.de.us/dnrec2000/>

Florida Department of Environmental Protection
Office of Wastewater Management
Twin Towers Office Building
2600 Blair Stone Road
Tallahassee, FL 32399-2400
Telephone: 850-921-9495
Web: <http://www.dep.state.fl.us/water>

Georgia Department of Natural Resources
Environmental Protection Division
4220 International Parkway, Suite 101
Atlanta Tradeport
Atlanta, GA 30354
Telephone: 404-362-4916
Web: <http://www.dnr.state.ga.us/dnr/environ/>

Hawaii Department of Health
Clean Water Branch
919 Ala Moana Boulevard, Room 301
Honolulu, HI 96814
Telephone: 808-586-4309
Web: <http://www.hawaii.gov/health/eh/cwb/forms/index.html>

Idaho (permitting authority is with the federal government)
US EPA Region 10
1200 Sixth Avenue
Seattle, WA 98101-1128
Telephone: 206-553-1448
Web: <http://yosemite.epa.gov/R10/ecocomm.nsf/0/
9e603fef1cccdcf9882569d90079cf55?OpenDocument>

Illinois Environmental Protection Agency
Bureau of Water
DWPC Permit Section 15
1021 North Grand Avenue East
P.O. Box 19276
Springfield, IL 62794-9276
Telephone: 217-782-3362
Web: <http://www.epa.state.il.us/water/forms.html>

Indiana Department of Environmental Management
Office of Water Quality
P.O. Box 6015
100 North Senate Avenue
Indianapolis, IN 46206-6015
Telephone: 317-232-8706
Web: <http://www.state.in.us/idem/owm/>

Iowa Department of Natural Resources
Environmental Protection Division
Wallace State Office Building
900 East Grand Avenue
Des Moines, IA 50319-0034
Telephone: 515-242-6128
Web: <http://www.state.ia.us/epd/wastewtr/feedlot/feedlt.htm>

Kansas Department of Health and Environment
Bureau of Water
1000 Southwest Jackson Street
Topeka, KS 66612-1367
Telephone: 785-296-0075
Web: <http://www.kdhe.state.ks.us/water/index.html>

Kentucky Department of Environmental Protection
Division of Water
14 Reilly Road
Frankfort, KY 40601
Telephone: 502-564-3410
Web: <http://water.nr.state.ky.us/dow/cafo.htm>

Louisiana Department of Environmental Quality
Office of Environmental Services
P.O. Box 82135
Baton Rouge, LA 70884
Telephone: 225-765-2215
Web: <http://www.deq.state.la.us/permits/index.htm>

Maine Department of Environmental Protection
Bureau of Land and Water Quality
17 State House Station
Augusta, ME 04333
Telephone: 207-287-7693
Web: <http://www.state.me.us/dep/blwq/ag.htm>

Maryland Department of the Environment
Water Management Administration
1800 Washington Boulevard
Baltimore, MD 21230
Telephone: 410-631-3567
Web: <http://www.mde.state.md.us/Water/index.asp>

Massachusetts (permitting authority is with the federal government)
US EPA Region 01
1 Congress Street, Suite 1100
Boston, MA 02114-2023
Telephone: 617-918-1875
Web: <http://cfpub2.epa.gov/npdes/
contacts.cfm?program_id=45&type=REGION>

Michigan Department of Environmental Quality
Water Division
P.O. Box 30273
Lansing, MI 48909
Telephone: 517-241-7832
Web: <http://www.michigan.gov/deq/1,1607,7-135-3313_3684—,00.html>

Minnesota Pollution Control Agency
Regional Environmental Management Division
520 Lafayette Road North
St. Paul, MN 55155-4194
Telephone: 651-296-7323
Web: <http://www.pca.state.mn.us/hot/feedlots.html#forms>

Mississippi Department of Environmental Quality
Office of Pollution Control
P.O. Box 10305
Jackson, MS 39289
Telephone: 601-961-5239
Web: <http://www.deq.state.ms.us/newweb/opchome.nsf/pages/opc>

Missouri Department of Natural Resources
Water Protection and Soil Conservation Division
P.O. Box 176
205 Jefferson Street
Jefferson City, MO 65102
Telephone: 573-751-1398
Web: <http://www.dnr.state.mo.us/oac/forms/index.htm>

Montana Department of Environmental Quality
Water Protection Bureau
P.O. Box 200901
1520 East Sixth Avenue
Helena, MT 59620
Telephone: 406-444-1454
Web: <http://www.deq.state.mt.us/wqinfo/Index.asp>

Nebraska Department of Environmental Quality
Water Quality Division
P.O. Box 98922
1200 N Street, Suite 400
Lincoln, NE 68509
Telephone: 402-471-4288
Web: <http://www.deq.state.ne.us>

Nevada Division of Environmental Protection
Bureau of Water Pollution Control
333 West Nye Lane, Suite 138
Carson City, NV 89706
Telephone: 775-687-9423
Web: <http://ndep.state.nv.us/index.htm>

New Hampshire Department of Environmental Services
P.O. Box 95
6 Hazen Drive
Concord, NH 03302-0095
Telephone: 603-271-2983
Web: <http://www.des.state.nh.us/water_intro.htm>

New Jersey Department of Environmental Protection
Division of Water Quality
P.O. Box 029
401 East State Street
Trenton, NJ 08625-0029
Telephone: 609-633-7021
Web: <http://www.state.nj.us/dep/dwq>

New Mexico (permitting authority is with the federal government)
US EPA Region 06
1445 Ross Avenue
Dallas, TX 75202-2733
Telephone: 214-665-7504
Web: <http://www.nmenv.state.nm.us/swqb/cafoq_a.html>

New York State Department of Environmental Conservation
Division of Water
625 Broadway
Albany, NY 12233
Telephone: 518-402-8117
Web: <http://www.dec.state.ny.us/website/dow/cafohome.html>

North Carolina Department of Environment and Natural Resources
Division of Water Quality
1617 Mail Service Center
Raleigh, NC 27699-1617
Telephone: 919-733-5083
Web: <http://h2o.enr.state.nc.us/index.html>

North Dakota State Department of Health
Division of Water Quality
1200 Missouri Avenue
Bismark, ND 58505-5520
Telephone: 701-328-5227
Web: <http://www.health.state.nd.us>

Ohio Environmental Protection Agency
Division of Surface Water
P.O. Box 1049
122 South Front Street
Columbus, OH 43224
Telephone: 614-644-2021
Web: <http://www.epa.state.oh.us/dsw/cafo>

Oklahoma (permitting authority is with the federal government)
US EPA Region 06
1445 Ross Avenue
Dallas, TX 75202-2733
Telephone: 214-665-7504
Web: <http://cfpub2.epa.gov/npdes/
contacts.cfm?program_id=45&type=REGION>

Oregon Department of Agriculture
Natural Resources Division
635 Capitol Street NE
Salem, OR 97301-2532
Telephone: 503-986-4700
Web: <http://www.oda.state.or.us/nrd/cafo/index.html>

Pennsylvania Department of Environmental Protection
Bureau of Water Supply and Wastewater Management
Rachel Carson State Office Building, 16th Floor
P.O. Box 8774
Harrisburg, PA 17105-8774
Telephone: 717-787-8184
Web: <http://www.dep.state.pa.us/dep/deputate/watermgt/wqp_wm/
cafo_home.htm>

Rhode Island Department of Environmental Management
Office of Water Resources
235 Promenade Street
Providence, RI 02908-5767
Telephone: 401-222-4700
Web: <http://www.state.ri.us/dem/programs/benviron/water/index.htm>

South Carolina Department of Health and Environmental Control
2600 Bull Street
Columbia, SC 29201
Telephone: 803-898-4167
Web: <http://www.scdhec.net/eqc/water/html/agcafo.html>

South Dakota Department of Environment and Natural Resources
Surface Water Quality
Joe Foss Building
523 E. Capitol Avenue
Pierre, SD 57501
Telephone: 605-773-3151
Web: <http://www.state.sd.us/denr/DES/Surfacewater/feedlotpermits.htm>

Tennessee Department of Environment and Conservation
Division of Water Pollution Control
6th Floor, L&C Annex
401 Church Street
Nashville, TN 37243
Telephone: 615-532-0652
Web: <http://www.state.tn.us/environment/permits/index.html>

Texas Natural Resource Conservation Commission
Texas Commission on Environmental Quality
P.O. Box 13087
Austin, TX 78711-3087
Telephone: 512-239-4480
Web: <http://www.tnrcc.state.tx.us/permitting/waterperm/wwperm/
tpdes.html#CAFO>

Utah Department of Environmental Quality
Division of Water Quality
P.O. Box 144870
Salt Lake City, UT 84114-4870
Telephone: 800-538-9251
Web: <http://waterquality.utah.gov>

Vermont Agency of Agriculture, Food, and Markets
116 State Street, Drawer 20
Montpelier, VT 05620-2901
Phone: (802) 828-2416
Web: <http://www.state.vt.us/agric/index.htm>

Virginia Department of Environmental Quality
P.O. Box 10009
Richmond, VA 23240-0009
Telephone: 804-698-4039
Web: <http://www.deq.state.va.us/>

Washington State Department of Ecology
Water Quality Program
P.O. Box 47600
Olympia, WA 98504-7600
Telephone: 360-407-6400
Web: <http://www.ecy.wa.gov/programs/wq/permits/index.html>

West Virginia Department of Environmental Protection
Division of Water Resources
1201 Greenbrier Street
Charleston, WV 25311-1088
Telephone: 304-558-2107
Web: <http://www.dep.state.wv.us/item.cfm?ssid=11>

Wisconsin Department of Natural Resources
Bureau of Watershed Management
P.O. Box 7921
101 South Webster Street
Madison, WI 53707
Telephone: 608-267-7651
Web: <http://www.dnr.state.wi.us/org/water/wm/ww/PmtTypes.htm>

Wyoming Department of Environmental Quality
Water Quality Division
Herschler Building
122 West 25th Street, 4th Floor
Cheyenne, WY 82009
Telephone: 307-777-7781
Web: <http://deq.state.wy.us/wqd/index.asp?pageid=5>

Appendix 2: State CAFO Regulations

State	Regulations
Alabama	Alabama Department of Environmental Management, chapter 355-6-7; <http://www.adem.state.al.us/Regulations/Div6a/Div6a> (viewed 6/18/03).
Alaska	See federal rules for EPA Region 10.
Arizona	Arizona Administrative Code R18-9-401 to -403; <http://www.sosaz.com/public_services/Title_18/18–09.pdf> (viewed 6/18/03).
Arkansas	Arkansas Pollution Control and Ecology Commission Regulation 5, <http://www.adeq.state.ar.us/regs/files/reg05_final_000323.pdf> (viewed 6/18/03).
California	California Code of Regulations, title 14, §§17823.1, 17823.5; title 23, §§2200, 2560, 2601, 3950; title 27, §20164; Statewide Water Quality Regulations for Confined Animal Facilities, subchapter 2, article 1, §§22560–65, <http://www.swrcb.ca.gov/~rwqcb5/available_documents/#confined> (viewed 6/18/03).
Colorado	Colorado Statutes §§25-8-501.1, 25-8-504; Code of Colorado Regulations, vol. 5, §§1002-81 and 1001-4 <http://www.cdphe.state.co.us/ap/hogfiles/hog_hom.html> (viewed 6/18/03).
Connecticut	Connecticut Department of Environmental Protection, Bureau of Water Management, Permitting, Enforcement and Remediation Division APP-110, Concentrated Animal Feeding Operations; Regulations of Connecticut State Agencies §22a-430-6(b).
Delaware	Delaware Code, title 3, §§2201–48, NPDES Form 2B Application, <http://www.dnrec.state.de.us/water2000/SiteMap/SiteMap1.asp?Type=FO> (viewed 6/18/03).
Florida	Florida Administrative Code, chapters 62-620, 62-660, 62-670, <http://www.dep.state.fl.us/water/wastewater/forms/pdf/620_3_.pdf> (viewed 6/18/03).

Georgia	Georgia Compilation Rules and Regulations, rules 391-3-6.19 (land application), 391-3-6.20 (swine), 391-3-6.21 (animal, nonswine), <http://www.dnr.state.ga.us/dnr/environ> (viewed 6/18/03).
Hawaii	Hawaii Administrative Rules, title 11, chapter 55, <http:// www.state.hi.us/health/rules/11-55.pdf> (viewed 6/18/03)— using federal EPA Form 3510-2B.
Idaho	See federal rules for EPA Region 10, Idaho Administrative Code, Agriculture rule 02.04.14, <http://www2.state.id.us/ adm/adminrules/rules/idapa02/0414.pdf> (dairy waste) (viewed 6/18/03); <http://www.agri.state.id.us/animal/ IBCECP.htm> (beef program) (viewed 6/18/03).
Illinois	Illinois Compiled Statutes Annotated, chapter 510, §§77/10–105, Illinois Administrative Code, title 35, parts 506, 560, 570, 580, <http://www.ipcb.state.il.us/SLR/ IPCBandIEPAEnvironmentalRegulations-Title35.asp> (viewed 6/18/03).
Indiana	Indiana Statutes Annotated §§13-18-10-1 to -10; Indiana Administrative Code, title 327, article 16, <http://www.in.gov/ idem/land/cfo/cforule.pdf> (viewed 6/18/03).
Iowa	Iowa Code §§171D.1–.4, 331.304A, 455B.109–.206, 455H.107, 455J.2, 654C.1–.11; Iowa Administrative Code rules 567-22, 567-23, 567-63, 567-64, 567-65, <http://www.state.ia.us/epd/ wastewtr/feedlot/567-65.pdf> (viewed 6/18/03), 567-72, chapter 567, appendix A <http://www.state.ia.us/epd/wastewtr/ feedlot/app-a.pdf> (viewed 6/18/03).
Kansas	Kansas Statutes, §§47-1501 to -1511; Kansas Administrative Regulations, title 28, articles 18 & 18a; §28-29-25d, <http:// www.kdhe.state.ks.us/feedlots/kdhelegis.htm> (viewed 6/18/ 03).
Kentucky	Kentucky Revised Statutes Annotated §224.10-100; Kentucky Administrative Regulations, title 401, chapter 5, section 005, <http://www.lrc.state.ky.us/kar/frntpage.htm> (viewed 6/18/ 03).
Louisiana	Louisiana Revised Statutes Annotated, title 33, §2335; Appendices to the Attorney General Statements for the LPDAS Program Submission, appendix B, <http://www.deq.state.la.us/ planning/regs/title33/index.htm> (viewed 6/18/03).
Maine	Maine Revised Statutes, title 7, §4201-14, <http:// janus.state.me.us/legis/statutes/7/title7ch747sec0.html> (viewed 6/18/03).

Maryland	Maryland Agriculture Code, §§8-704.1, 8-704.2, 8-801 to -807; Code of Maryland Regulations, title 15, subtitle 20 (nutrient management), Maryland Concentrated Animal Feeding Operations General Permit no.96-AF, <http://www.mde.state.md.us/Permits/WaterManagementPermits/water_applications/animalFeed.asp> (viewed 6/18/03).
Massachusetts	See federal rules for EPA Region 1, <http://www.epa.gov/NE/npdes/contacts.html> (viewed 6/18/03).
Michigan	Michigan Administrative Code, part 21, §323.2101–.2192, <http://www.michigan.gov/deq/0,1607,7-135-3307_4132-14902-,00.html#Water> (viewed 6/19/03).
Minnesota	Minnesota Statutes Annotated §§17.136, 115.076, 116.06, 116.07; Minnesota Rules chapter 7020, <http://www.revisor.leg.state.mn.us/arule/7020/> (viewed 6/18/03).
Mississippi	Mississippi Code Annotated §49-17-29; <http://opc.deq.state.ms.us/epd/whatform.asp> (viewed 6/18/03)—listing EPA Form 3510-2B for use.
Missouri	Missouri Revised Statutes §§640.700–.758, 644.016–.053; Missouri Code of State Regulations, title 10, division 20, chapter 14, <http://www.sos.state.mo.us/adrules/csr/current/10csr/10c20-14.pdf> (viewed 6/18/03).
Montana	Montana Code Annotated §§81-3-201, 81-3-202; Montana Administrative Rules, rules 17-30-1301 et. seq.; Montana Administrative Rules, rules 17-30-1601 et. seq.; <http://www.deq.state.mt.us/wqinfo/MPDES/CAFO.asp> (viewed 6/18/03).
Nebraska	Nebraska Revised Statutes §§54-2401 to -2409; Nebraska Administrative Rules and Regulations, title 130, chapter 2, <http://www.deq.state.ne.us/> (viewed 6/18/03).
Nevada	Nevada Administrative Code, chapter 445A, §§228-263; state working with the federal government, see <http://www.epa.gov/region09/cross_pr/animalwaste/nevada.html> (viewed 6/18/03).
New Hampshire	New Hampshire Revised Statutes Annotated, title 40, §431.35.
New Jersey	New Jersey Administrative Code, title 7, §14A-1.1 through 14A-4.9; <http://www.rci.rutgers.edu/~axellute/rullaw/njlaw.html> (viewed 6/18/03).
New Mexico	See federal rules for EPA Region 6.
New York	New York Soil and Water Conservation Districts Law §11-b; New York Department of Environmental Conservation General Permit GP-99-01, <http://www.dec.state.ny.us/website/dow/cafohome.html> (viewed 6/18/03).

North Carolina   North Carolina Administrative Code, title 15A, chapter 02, subchapters B, D, and H, <http://ncrules.state.nc.us/> (viewed 6/18/03).

North Dakota   North Dakota Administrative Code, chapter 33-16-03, <http:/ /www.state.nd.us/lr/information/acdata/html/33-16.html> (viewed 6/18/03).

Ohio   Ohio Administrative Code §§1501:15-5-01 to -07, <http:// onlinedocs.andersonpublishing.com/oac/> (viewed 6/18/03).

Oklahoma   Oklahoma Statutes, title 2, §§9-200 to -215, 10-9.3 to -9.24; title 27A, §3-2-109; title 82, §§1020.11a and 1020.12; Oklahoma Administrative Code, title 35, chapters 17, subchapters 3 and 5, <http://www.state.ok.us/%7Eokag/main/srvs/ agform/crules.pdf> (viewed 6/18/03).

Oregon   Oregon Revised Statutes, §§468B.050 to .230, 537.141, 537.545, 561.175; Oregon Administrative Rules, rules 340-051-0005 to -0080, <http://arcweb.sos.state.or.us/rules/ OARS_300/OAR_340/340_051.html> (viewed 6/18/03).

Pennsylvania   Pennsylvania Statutes, title 3, §§1701–18; Pennsylvania Code, chapter 92.5a, <http://www.pacode.com/secure/data/025/ chapter92/s92.5a.html> (viewed 6/18/03); see also <http:// www.dep.state.pa.us/dep/deputate/watermgt/wqp/ wqp_wm/cafo_home.htm> (viewed 6/18/03).

Rhode Island   Regulations for the Rhode Island Pollutant Discharge Elimination System, rule 27, <http://www.state.ri.us/dem/pubs/ regs/REGS/WATER/RIPDES.pdf> (viewed 6/18/03).

South Carolina   South Carolina Code §§47-20-10 to -170; South Carolina Department of Health and Environmental Control, rule 61-43.

South Dakota   South Dakota Codified Laws, §§34A-2-40, 34A-3A-44; South Dakota Administrative Rules, article 74:52:02:30, <http:// www.state.sd.us/denr/denr_rule_numerical.htm> (viewed 6/ 18/03).

Tennessee   Tennessee Code Annotated, §§44-5-101 to -108 (transferred); Tennessee Department of Environment and Conservation, chapter 1200-4-10, <http://www.state.tn.us/environment/ wpc/cafo_gp6.htm> (viewed 6/18/03); see also <http:// www.state.tn.us/environment/permits/cafo.htm> (viewed 11/8/02).

Texas   Texas Administrative Code, title 30, chapters 116, 321 (subchapter B); see Texas Natural Resources Conservation Commission TNRCC-0728; <http://www.tnrcc.state.tx.us/permitting/waterperm/wwperm/cafo.html> (viewed 6/18/03).

Utah	Utah Administrative Code, rule 317-8-3.5; see Utah Depart-
	ment of Environmental Quality Permit No. UTG 130000,
	<http://waterquality.utah.gov/updes/
	fish_hatch_permit.pdf> (viewed 6/18/03).
Vermont	Vermont Statutes Annotated, title 6, §§4849–55; Vermont
	Large Farm Operation Regulations, <http://www.state.vt.us/
	agric/lforules.htm> (viewed 6/18/03).
Virginia	Virginia Code §§62.1-44.15 to .30; Virginia Administrative
	Code, title 9, section 25-32-250; <http://www.deq.state.va.us/
	pdf/watrregs/vpa.pdf> (viewed 11/8/002).
Washington	Washington Revised Code Annotated §§90.48, 90.64; <http:/
	/www.ecy.wa.gov/programs/wq/dairy/index.html> (viewed
	6/18/03).
West Virginia	West Virginia Code of State Rules, §§47-10-13.1, 47-10 appen-
	dix B; <http://129.71.220.230/csr/
	rules.asp?Agency=Water%20Resources> (viewed 6/19/03).
Wisconsin	Wisconsin Statutes Annotated, §§281.1, 283.91; Wisconsin
	Administrative Code, Agriculture, Trade and Development,
	chapters 12, 50, 60; Wisconsin Administrative Code, NR 243;
	<http://www.dnr.state.wi.us/org/water/wm/ww/
	statauth.htm> (viewed 6/18/03).
Wyoming	Wyoming Water Quality Rules and Regulations, chapter 3
	and 11, <http://deq.state.wy.us/wqd/index.asp?pageid=115>
	(viewed 6/18/03).

Index

accepted agricultural practices, 105, 107
accountability, 161
AFOs: abating pollution at, 128; concentrations at, 7, 134; definition of, 51; insufficient regulation of, 137; as non-point sources, 136; and pollution, 143; production of, 31; regulating, 133–34; regulations for, 135–36, 178–82; smells from, 104; violations by, 135
agencies: assisting producers, 151; for CAFOs, 169–77; enforcement, 137–38, 139, 162; failure to enforce of, 140, 141, 142, 143
agricultural assistance programs, 164
agricultural manufacturing, 107
agricultural pollutants, 2
Agricultural Stabilization and Conservation Service, 95, 99
agricultural storm-water discharges, 56
agricultural subsidies, 165
agriculture: agenda of, 2; changes to, 15, 146, 152, 159; and democracy, 10; districts designated for, 106; and exemptions, 11; future of, 160; innovation in, 15; and production changes, 15; progress in, 3; public goods and, 147; public support for, 147; status of, 11
agronomic practices, 81
agronomic rates, 65
air resources, 164, 166
American Farm Bureau Federation, 16
American Humane Association, 43
American Medical Association, 39
ammonia, 38, 70
animal production, 21
animals: code of ethics for, 43; concentrations of, 2, 21-22, 26, 31, 50; confined, 3, 8, 21; factories producing, 6; housing for, 58; mistreatment of, 43; numbers of, 22; numbers of, for CAFOs, 51–52; pollution from, 4, 44; and problems from confinement, 43; rights of, 43; states

producing, 22; suffering, 43; in waters, 79; waste from, 33; welfare of, 42–43
antibiotics, 10, 19, 39–40, 44
attitudes, changing, 10
attorney general: private, 142; state, 139, 141
attorneys' fees, 143

bankruptcy, 16
best management practices. *See* BMPs
biodiversity, 10, 77, 86
biotechnology, 23, 26
birds, 9, 10
blue-baby syndrome, 41
BMPs: advocating, 150–51; costs of, 81; definition of, 81; minimizing water pollution through, 81; for odor reduction, 71; training for, 66
Bormann lawsuit, 111–12
bovine spongiform encephalopathy, 42, 155
British Royal Society for the Prevention of Cruelty to Animals, 43–44
broilers, 31
buffer(s): cleansing aspects of, 84, 86; costs of, 80; riparian, 80, 84
buffer zones, 64

CAFOs: classification as point sources, 50; definition of, 51–52; designated, 52; enforcing regulations of, 138; large, 51-52, 55; and lawsuits, 143; medium, 52; as nuisances, 114; number of, permitted, 53; and nutrient-management plans, 55; regulations for, 133–35, 151–52, 156; and setbacks, 55; small, 52; state agencies overseeing, 169–77; violations of regulations by, 161
Campylobacter, 39, 41
cattle, numbers, 22, 31
Centers for Disease Control, 41
certification: for AFOs, 135; in general, 65–

TERENCE J. CENTNER, a professor at the University of Georgia's College of Agriculture and Environmental Sciences, grew up on a diary and fruit farm in New York State and was active in the 4-H club program. He studied agriculture at Cornell University and graduated with distinction. Further studies led to a J.D. degree from the State University of New York at Buffalo and an LL.M. in agricultural law from the University of Arkansas.

Terry has analyzed a wide variety of topics relating agricultural production with economic performance and environmental quality to advocate new strategies for resolving conflicts and preserving resources. His research findings, published in more than 95 journal articles and 100 other publications, have been used by fellow researchers, policy makers, and legislatures in devising new regulations to improve economic performance and environmental quality.

At Georgia Terry serves as his college's prelaw adviser and teaches environmental and public-health law courses. He received his university's Study in a Second Discipline Award and his college's Alumni Research Award.

Terry served as secretary-treasurer and president of the American Agricultural Law Association. His teaching and research programs have been recognized internationally through his selection as an Alexander von Humbolt Research Fellow at the University of Göttingen and a Fulbright Senior Scholar at the University of Mannheim and via lectures in various foreign countries.

The University of Illinois Press
is a founding member of the
Association of American University Presses.

Composed in 9.5/13 Stone Serif
with New Caledonia display
by Jim Proefrock
at the University of Illinois Press
Designed by Paula Newcomb
Manufactured by Thomson-Shore, Inc.

University of Illinois Press
1325 South Oak Street
Champaign, IL 61820-6903
www.press.uillinois.edu